Sun at Midnight

Books by W.S. Merwin

POEMS

The Shadow of Sirius
Selected Poems (U.K.)
Present Company
Migration: New & Selected Poems
The Pupil
The River Sound
The Folding Cliffs: A Narrative
Flower & Hand
The Vixen
The Second Four Books of Poems
Travels
Selected Poems
The Rain in the Trees
Opening the Hand
Finding the Islands
Feathers from the Hill
The Compass Flower
The First Four Books of Poems
Writings to an Unfinished Accompaniment
The Carrier of Ladders
The Lice
The Moving Target
The Drunk in the Furnace
Green with Beasts
The Dancing Bears
A Mask for Janus

PROSE

The Book of Fables
Summer Doorways: A Memoir
The Ends of the Earth: Essays
The Mays of Ventadorn
The Lost Upland: Stories of
    Southwest France
Unframed Originals: Recollections
Houses and Travellers
The Miner's Pale Children

TRANSLATIONS

Collected Haiku of Yosa Buson
    (with Takako Lento)
Selected Translations 1948–2011
Sir Gawain & the Green Knight
Purgatorio
East Window: The Asian
    Translations
Pieces of Shadow: Selected Poems of
    Jaime Sabines
Sun at Midnight (Poems by
    Musō Soseki) (with Sōiku
    Shigematsu)
Vertical Poetry (Poems by
    Roberto Juarroz)
From the Spanish Morning
Four French Plays

Euripedes' Iphigeneia at Aulis (with
    George E. Dimock Jr.)
Osip Mandelstam: Selected Poems
    (with Clarence Brown)
Asian Figures
Transparence of the World
    (Poems by Jean Follain)
Voices (Poems by Antonio Porchia)
Products of the Perfected Civilization
    (Selected Writings of Chamfort)
Twenty Love Poems and a
    Song of Despair (Poems by
    Pablo Neruda)
The Song of Roland
Lazarillo de Tormes
Spanish Ballads
The Satires of Persius
Poem of the Cid

ANTHOLOGY

Lament for the Makers:
    A Memorial Anthology

Musō Soseki

SUN AT MIDNIGHT

Poems and Letters

•••

Translated by W.S. Merwin
and Sōiku Shigematsu

Copper Canyon Press
Port Townsend, Washington

Copper Canyon Press thanks Emiko Ebara and John Bednarik for their assistance in Japan.

Copper Canyon Press is in residence at Fort Worden State Park in Port Townsend, Washington, under the auspices of Centrum. Centrum is a gathering place for artists and creative thinkers from around the world, students of all ages and backgrounds, and audiences seeking extraordinary cultural enrichment.

LIBRARY OF CONGRESS CATALOGING-IN-PUBLICATION DATA

Musō Soseki, 1275–1351.
[Works. Selections. English]
Sun at midnight / Musō Soseki ; translated by W.S. Merwin and Sōiku Shigematsu.
    pages   cm
Includes bibliographical references and index.
ISBN 978-1-55659-439-7 (pbk.)
1. Musō Soseki, 1275–1351 — Translations into English. 2. Buddhist sermons, Japanese — Translations into English. 3. Zen Buddhism — Sermons. I. Merwin, W.S. (William Stanley), 1927– translator.
II. Shigematsu, Sōiku, 1943– translator. III. Title.
PL792.M87A2 2013'
895.6'12 — dc23

                                                        2012045655

98765432 FIRST PRINTING

COPPER CANYON PRESS
Post Office Box 271
Port Townsend, Washington 98368
www.coppercanyonpress.org

Contents

Introduction   *xiii*

Wandering   *3*
A Lodging House in Town   *4*
Buddha's Satori   *5*
For Taihei Oshō   *6*
Rinzan Oshō Visits Me   *7*
"I'm not so deep in it"   *8*
Reply to Rinzan Oshō   *9*
Thanks for Daisen Oshō's Visit   *11*
"Chick feed is what I eat"   *13*
"Loud thunder"   *14*
Thanks Sent to Taihei Oshō   *15*
From My Hut in Miura   *16*
"In these mountain villages and harbor towns"   *17*
"From the beginning"   *18*
"East of the strait"   *19*
"My thatched hut"   *20*
"All on my own I'm happy"   *21*
Heaven Peak   *22*
Gem Mountain   *23*
Another Summit   *24*

Bamboo Garden   25

To the Emperor's Messenger   26

Old Creek   27

Snow Valley   28

Dry Tree   29

Old Man in Retirement   30

Strange Peak   31

Poem on Dry Mountain (a Zen Garden)   32

At the Nachi Kannon Hall   33

Spring Cliff   34

Reply to Gen'nō Oshō's Poem   35

For the Death of a Monk   36

"People's abuse"   37

To Kengai Oshō of Engaku-ji   38

Moon Mountain   39

Free Old Man   40

Visiting My Old Hut in Late Spring   41

"On the blue waves"   42

Laughing Mountain   43

Inauguration of Fukusan Dormitory   44

Cloud Mountain   45

At Gen's Embarkation for Yuan China   46

At Kan's Embarkation for Yuan China   47

At Iku's Embarkation for Yuan China   48

Mourning for the Layman Named Cloud Peak   49

Patriarch Peaks   50

East Peak   51

Old Hut   52

Tengan Oshō's Visit to Erin-ji   53

LIVING IN THE MOUNTAINS: TEN POEMS

"In this small hut"   57

"Among rocks and valleys"   58

"Very high this mountain"   59

"All worries and troubles"   60

"A curtain of cloud hangs"   61

"Don't ask suspiciously"   62

"I wake from my noon nap"   63

"Green mountains"   64

"Time for a walk"   65

"With compassionate hands"   66

◆◆◆

Pine Shade   69

Plum Window   70

Jewel Field   71

Truth Hall   72

No Precedent   73

Old Man To-The-Point   74

Old Man Advancing   75

Abiding Mountain   76

Snow Garden   77

One Hut   78

Moon Tree Cliff   79

Gem Creek   80

No-Word Hut   81

Old Mountain   82

No End Point   83

Lover of Mountains   84

Sūzan Oshō's Visit   85

Reply to Sūzan Oshō's Snow Poem   86

The Pure Sound Gate of the Riverside Temple   87

For Gen the New Head Priest of Erin-ji   88

For Myō's Departure for Anzen-ji   89

For Myō's Departure for Shōfuku-ji   90

For Tetsu the New Head Priest of Erin-ji   91

For Shō the New Head Priest of Erin-ji   92

At Whole-World-In-View Hut   93

Ashikaga Tadayoshi's Palace   94

Climbing Down the Snowy Mountain   95

Snow at Rōhatsu Sesshin   96

It   97

Magnificent Peak   98

Reply to Bukkō Zenji's Poem at Seiken-ji   99

Snow   100

Gem Forest   101

Withered Zen   102

The Fragrance of the Udumbara *103*

House of Spring *104*

No Gain *105*

Seashore *106*

For Ko Who Has Come Back from China *107*

TEN SCENES IN THE DRAGON OF HEAVEN TEMPLE

The Gate of Universal Light *111*

Incomparable-Verse Valley *112*

Hall of the Guardian God *113*

Hui-neng's Pond *114*

The Peak of the Held-Up Flower *115*

The Bridge Where the Moon Crosses *116*

Three-Step Waterfall *117*

Cave of the Thousand Pines *118*

Dragon-Gate House *119*

Turtle Head Stupa *120*

◆◆◆

Tiger Valley *123*

Tōki-no-Ge (Satori Poem) *124*

The Garden at the General's Residence *125*

Temple of Eternal Light *126*

Mugoku Oshō's Snow Poem *127*

Sūzan Oshō's Visit to My West Mountain Hut *128*

On the Wall of Cloud-Friend Hut   129
Digging Out the Buddha Relic   130
Reply to a Friend's Poem   131
Ox Turned Loose   132
Clear Valley   133
Old Man at Leisure   134
Ancient Origin   135
Old Man of Few Words   136
Jewel Cliff   137
Joy Mountain   138
For a Monk Going West   139
Flat Mountain   140
Beyond the World   141
Beyond Light   142
Hut in Harmony   143
Lamenting the Civil War   144

LETTERS

West Mountain Evening Talk   149
On Gardens and the Way   175
Musō's Admonition   181

List of Names   183
Notes to the Poems   189
About the Translator   195

xii

Introduction

Everything that remains to our world of the many talents of the man known to us as Musō Soseki is addressed to our most intimate nature, and yet we approach him now, from wherever we are, over vast distances.

He was born ten years after Dante, in 1275 according to our reckoning, which was not the reckoning in his birthplace in the province of Ise, on the coast far to the west of the capital of Japan, then named Edo. The forested province of Ise had been the home for over a thousand years of one of the most revered shrines of Shinto, the one that houses the legendary mirror of the sun goddess Amaterasu, a mythological ancestor of the emperor. The shrine itself and the compound are, as they were when Musō was born, a celebrated example of a pure form of Japanese architecture known as the Divine Style — plain, archaic, severe, and elegant, its origins linked to the worship of trees and the building of ships, and to the defining of enclosed clearings in the forest in order to establish, with a ritual use of space, gardens.

This practice, and the legends that emanated from it, must have been part of the familiar world around Musō in his first years. He may have been taken to the great shrine as an infant. Certainly he saw, then or later, others built on the same pattern, and the images they presented to him would have made a deep impression on a child who was to become one of the great garden designers of Japan.

But his parents were Buddhists, his mother a devout worshiper of the bodhisattva Avalokiteshvara, the representation of compassion. The tradition of medieval Buddhist hagiography is stiff with conventions, as other hagiographical traditions are, and some of its accounts are legends. A few that came to embroider what was remembered of the life of Musō seem familiar, like recurrent dreams. It was told that Musō's mother had prayed to Avalokiteshvara for a child, and had dreamed one night of a golden light flowing into her mouth. It was a full thirteen months later, however, before Musō was born.

His third year, according to the history, was one of loss. His family moved away from Ise to the province of Kai, and in August of that year his mother died. Those familiar with the life and writings of Dōgen Zenji (1200–1253) will recall that Dōgen's mother died when Dōgen was eight years old, and that her death—and the sight of the smoke of the incense burning beside her body—became the first recognizable step toward his own religious realization. Dōgen had lost his father at the age of three. There is a tradition in Zen, and in Buddhism in general, of children who were foundlings, or orphans, or who were given up to temples at a very early age, and Musō combined these. During the year after the death of his mother he is said to have shown a precocious religious fervor, reciting sutras and prayers before the Buddhist images. A religious life was predicted for him and then probably was expected of him. He was a particularly gentle child who avoided arguments and shunned contention of any kind, even rough games with children of his own age. When he was nine his father took him to the Shingon temple in Kai and gave him up to the religious life.

There Musō became a student of Mantrayana Buddhism, returning only on occasional visits to see his father and stepmother. She cooked sumptuous meals to celebrate his being at home, and when he went back to the temple he took some of her delicious food with him to share with his friends, who probably subsisted most of the time on rice and tea. So she invited him to bring his friends home with him. One day he saw someone nearby eating a rich dinner while his servants ate almost nothing, and he resolved that if ever he had servants, their food would not differ from his own.

At eighteen he went to Nara to take his vows as a monk and have his head shaved. After that he devoted himself entirely to the study of Buddhist texts, until one day he was present at the death, in great anguish of spirit, of a learned Buddhist, who had been a noted authority of esoteric Buddhism and Tendai metaphysics, and had preached for years on Buddhist doctrine. Musō was shaken to see that all this man had known about Buddhism had helped him so little at the moment of his death. He had heard of a school of Buddhism that was based upon a "special transmission outside the scriptures" and he determined to learn about it. When he was not yet twenty he left the Shingon sect and became a student of Zen at Ken'nin-ji in Kyoto, and then at Engaku-ji and Kenchō-ji in Kamakura.

The director of Kenchō-ji was a Chinese monk named Issan who had recently arrived (1299) in Japan to escape the Mongol occupation of China. He became Musō's teacher, and Musō remained with him, practicing fervently, for a number of years. As he did, his doubt, his anxiety at his own lack of realization and clarity, grew until one day in desperation he said to Issan, "I cannot attain enlightenment. Show it to me."

Issan said, "There is no word in our school. There is no rule to transmit."

"Show me your compassion and your way."

"There is no compassion. And there is not any way."

Musō decided that there was no point in remaining

with Issan and he went to the nearby temple of Engaku-ji. Master Kōhō-Ken'nichi there, a pupil at one time of another Chinese master, was famous for his insight. Musō went to see him and repeated his final conversation with Issan to Kōhō, who answered, "You should have said to Issan, 'Teacher, you have revealed too much.'" At these words Musō is said to have had a faint glimpse of the realization he was seeking, but he knew it was no more than that. He set out on a pilgrimage to the north. He spent the summer of 1305, his thirtieth year, in Zen practice in a hermitage in the province of Jōshū. One night he sat out in the garden where there was a cool breeze. Very late, he rose to go back into the hermitage. He had no light, but the place was so familiar that he thought he knew exactly where he was, and he reached out to steady himself against a wall. But the wall was not there and he fell. Suddenly he burst out laughing, for he felt the anguish and intense searching of so many years suddenly dissolved. He wrote his *tōki-no-ge*, or satori poem, and in the autumn took it to Kōhō, who questioned him and gave the seal of his approval to Musō's realization. Musō remained with Kōhō, and three years later Kōhō transmitted to him his own dead master's robe, making Musō his successor.

But Musō was not drawn to the courtly and hierar-chical world of official Zen. He left Kamakura and spent most of the next twenty years in remote temples and hermitages in the provinces, practicing Zen to clarify and deepen his insight. Yet despite his avoidance of the centers of fashion and influence, his reputation grew, and in 1325 Emperor Go-Daigo appointed Musō to the temple of Nanzen-ji in Kyoto, one of the most important and revered Zen temples in Japan, and there the emperor himself became a student of Musō. In 1329 the shogun appointed him to the temple of Engaku-ji, and Musō returned to Kamakura.

Japan at the time was torn by civil wars. The imperial power had eroded and passed into the hands of the warlords of Kamakura. Emperor Go-Daigo was anxious to regain the lost power of the throne, and the result was a series of fierce and devastating campaigns. In 1334 the emperor brought Musō back from Kamakura to Nanzen-ji. But in the following years the warrior lords rose to power and the emperor took refuge in a temple on Mount Hiei. Musō retired from his position at Nanzen-ji and took up residence at the smaller temple of Rinsen-ji, by the Ōi River on the west of Kyoto. In June of 1336 Ashikaga Takauji entered Kyoto in triumph and became the first of the Ashikaga dynasty, which was to endure through fifteen generations, during almost two and a half centuries.

Musō was already known to the new ruler, who was himself a dedicated student of Buddhism. Takauji and his brother, Tadayoshi, both had consulted Musō on religious matters, and they continued to do so once they were in power. Takauji's written questions to Musō, and Musō's replies, were later assembled and edited by one of Musō's successors to form the volume known as *Muchū Mondō, Dialogues in the Dream*. Takauji, like Musō's mother, was particularly devoted to the veneration of the bodhisattva of compassion, Avalokiteshvara. Not at ease in the world of power and conflict, he cherished a wish to retire from it altogether, and two years after his triumphal entry into Kyoto he turned over his duties to his brother Tadayoshi and devoted himself to the study of the Buddha dharma.

Takauji was tormented by the thought of the many who had suffered and died because of the civil wars in which he had played so important a part. At Musō's suggestion he founded Ankoku-ji, "temples of peace," and his brother built Rishō-tō, a Buddhist stupa.

The wave of temple building brought into play some of Musō's own talents. In his midsixties, in 1339, he was consulted in the restoration of the temple of Saihō-ji and its garden in the western part of Kyoto. The original temple had been built six hundred years earlier by a Buddhist monk, and at one time many buildings had occupied the site, but the entire temple had been destroyed during one of the periods of civil wars that had ravaged Japan.

The patron of the restored Saihō-ji and its garden was a nobleman named Nakahara no Chikahide, and the garden that Musō designed for the temple became famous in the history of Japanese gardens and of Japanese Buddhism.

In Japan gardens and religious observance had been closely associated for a very long time, and the boundary between architecture and gardens was indefinite. The formal compound of a Shinto temple, its ground covered with pebbles, is at once part of the enclosed structure surrounding the sacred tree and a garden, an ancestor of the raked-gravel gardens of the Zen tradition. The art of gardening had assumed as natural a role in Japanese religious custom as the arts of painting and sculpture, architecture and chant. It was not conceived of simply as a decorative addition to a place of human use. In the settings of Shinto and of Japanese Buddhism, it suggests, and is meant to exemplify, a view of being.

The gardens of the Pure Land sect of Buddhism, which had been established in Japan almost three centuries before Musō's birth, were intended to evoke the paradise of Amida (Amitābha) Buddha, the Buddha of the setting sun and the hereafter. The veneration of Amida

Buddha and the hope for his western paradise fostered an iconography that derived from images of the court and from the tantric mandalas of Shingon Buddhism; and the gardens of the Jōdo sect, as it came to be called (from Saihō Jōdo, the Pure Land of the West), were conceived as mandalas symbolizing paradise. Because they were also the residences of the noblemen who commissioned them, these wealthy and powerful few were already dwelling — at least in principle — in the paradise to come. The gardens were inevitably extremely formal and symmetrical; their shapes and their structures were manifestations of courtly elegance. Temple buildings and residences alike perpetuated traditional court architecture, and the gardens made characteristic use of bodies of water to provide, from different viewpoints, the illusion of distance and the sense that objects, perspectives, and edifices were floating on their own reflections.

This use of water in the Jōdo gardens in turn had its origin in the Heian court gardens, the "dream gardens," of the ninth century, with their emphasis on artificial lakes and streams. And before the Heian lake gardens there were, of course, the formal lake gardens of China with their carefully composed views of water and islands, their bridges and standing rocks. In the mid-ninth century the nobility began to plan gardens that deliberately evoked the wilder landscapes of other parts of Japan. Peninsulas planted with trees reached out into lakes. Lakeshores were covered with pebbles to represent ocean beaches. The attempt to suggest living landscapes worked against the urge for symmetrical formality and helped to lighten it and render its symbolism subtler and more complex. By the eleventh century the principles of the Heian gardens — conceived then, of course, as the correct principles for all gardens — were established conventions that could be summarized in *Treatise on Garden Making* by Tachibana Toshitsuna, the son of an important political figure of the period. Toshitsuna set forth the rules for making ponds, lakes, and waterfalls, and for arranging and planting trees and growing things, all with a doctrinaire finality that includes his detailed predictions of the catastrophes awaiting heretics who might presume to do things in any other way. The rules of Heian gardening had become superstitions, and some of this development may have derived from elements of Chinese geomancy whose meanings, by Toshitsuna's period, were no longer clearly remembered.

We do not know what Musō had learned of the art of garden design by the time he undertook to design the garden of Saihō-ji, but he was surely acquainted with the main currents of these traditions and must have been familiar with many court and temple gardens. Saihō-ji combines aspects of the paradise gardens of the Jōdo sect with far fewer of the symmetrical inventions generally considered manifestations of the spirit of Zen. There is a lake with an island in it, and a wandering series of rocks. A path meanders along the winding lakeshore.

One of the conditions, one of the materials, indeed, of the art of gardening, whatever gardeners may think of it, is the role of change, which makes gardening particularly appropriate to Buddhism. Nothing stays as the hand of the gardener leaves it or as the mind of the gardener originally conceives of it, and although Musō in his gardens made extensive and original use of such things as rocks, which change so slowly that they can be taken as symbols of permanence, those gardens of his that later generations saw and see are inevitably different from those he would have seen in his lifetime. Trees and all living things there have grown, died, been replaced. Shadows and leaves fall differently even in those gardens that have been cared for and kept as close as possible to the way he designed them. Saihō-ji itself is famous for, among other things, something that has changed enormously since the time of Musō's original garden and, in the view of most commentators, could have had no place in his plan. The ground under the trees by the lake, and in other sections of the garden reached by stone steps, is covered with a profusion of different mosses that curl like waves around the arrangements of large stones on the upper levels. It is said that these celebrated mosses, or at least many of them, spread through parts of the garden only in the nineteenth century when the temple became too poor to be able to maintain the garden. Yet there may well have been some mosses in the original plan. For instance, up on the hillside there is a detail that recurs in a number of Musō's gardens, a dry waterfall in which large vertical stones suggest the cascading of water. And at the foot of the stone waterfall there is a basin brimming not with water but with moss.

In the same year that the garden at Saihō-ji was laid out, perhaps on the site of an earlier garden, Emperor Go-Daigo died. Musō urged the Ashikagas, Takauji and Tadayoshi, to build a temple dedicated to the spirit of the dead emperor whom they had deposed, a project that might help to restore harmony between the old dynasty and the new one. The site chosen had once been an imperial estate, with a Heian lake garden. Musō's plans transformed it into the present temple enclosure and garden of Tenryū-ji, a labor that took five years. Parts of the garden appear in some of Musō's poems — its dry waterfall; its lake, named Hui-neng's Pond after the Sixth Zen Patriarch; its West Mountains (Arashiyama). It combines a great sweep of landscape and sense of space with feelings of intimacy and simplicity. Along with Zuisen-ji in Kamakura, with its cave and ponds, and the pond garden at Kenchō-ji in Kamakura, it is considered one of the works that best exemplifies Musō's conception and style of garden design. Perhaps appropriate to the vision of emptiness that he himself taught in all his arts, his very role in its plan has been disputed, though there is a record of Ashikaga Takauji's directive to him to turn the old imperial estate into a temple compound.

Musō's work on gardens filled the last decade of his life. He managed to combine it with teaching and advisory and administrative duties. In his late years he settled in the small riverside temple of Rinsen-ji, on the Ōi River at the edge of Kyoto. Once an imperial villa, Rinsen-ji had been converted into a temple by Emperor Go-Daigo as a shrine for his second son, who had died there. The emperor had made Musō the temple's first abbot, as Musō was later to become the first abbot of Tenryū-ji, and at Rinsen-ji too Musō redesigned the garden. But at Rinsen-ji his work has completely disappeared, as a result of war and neglect. The present garden there, a stone and gravel enclosure in the style of the famous one at Ryōan-ji, across the city, is a modern addition.

It was at Rinsen-ji, on September 29, 1351, that Musō wrote a final poem:

> In the real world
>> the pure world
>>> no separation exists

why wait
          for another time
                    and another meaning
of the teaching
          on Vulture Peak
                    is here today
who else
          are you looking for
                    to preserve the Way?

He died on the following day, September 30, at the age
of seventy-seven. Cremation was not then the invari-
able rule for the disposal of bodies, and Musō was bur-
ied at the end of the main hall of worship. The slabs of
rock covering his tomb, which can be seen from outside
the building, lie under the floor of the shrine; a rock for-
mation beside them resembles a chain of mountains in
a Sung dynasty painting. Over the tomb, two fluores-
cent light tubes have been attached to the beams under
the floor. Above, in the raised shrine, is a wooden statue
of Musō that looks life-size. He is seated in what is no
doubt zazen posture. The carved robes flow down from
the raised seat to the floor. His hands are in the medi-
tation mudra and his eyes are half-closed. One can see
even in the likeness the gentleness that distinguished
him as a child.

Musō had had some 13,145 recorded students: monks,
nuns, and laity, including seven emperors. Fifty-two of

his students received his approval as successors and a number of them in turn became renowned teachers. He had founded fourteen temples in Kyoto, Kamakura, and other parts of Japan. Upon his death, his writings, collected by his followers, included three volumes of conversations, which became *Dialogues in the Dream*, a volume of sermons, and the volume of poems from which the present translation was made.

The arts that Musō practiced — poetry, painting, calligraphy, garden design — depended, as all arts do, on a balance of convention and control, on the one hand, and spontaneity on the other. There is an inevitable tension between the two elements, and yet ideally the two seem to give life to each other and become one. The gardens with their varying evocations of what is considered natural are elaborately controlled manifestations of the conventions that Musō inherited and developed, though Musō is said to have favored a freer and less artificial style than was fashionable in his day.

His poetry was written both in Japanese and in Chinese, in two traditional forms, more than half of it in the gāthās — four-line Chinese verses — that had become conventional in the world of Zen in China before Zen passed to Japan. It was customary for students of Ch'an, as the teaching was called in China, to write a verse to express what they had understood, after they had had what they considered to be an experience of satori, or insight into the nature of reality. The custom was established by the time of the *Platform Sutra of the Sixth Patriarch* in the latter part of the eighth century. In that important Zen text a crucial turn of the story of the Sixth Patriarch depends upon two gāthās, the first composed by a monk at the Fifth Patriarch's monastery, which translates:

> The body is the Bodhi tree
> The mind is a clear mirror
> Always keep the mirror polished
> Let no dust gather on it

The other gāthā, attributed by legend to the Sixth Patriarch, survives in various forms. The most famous of them might be translated:

> Bodhi has no tree
> The mirror rests on nothing
> From the beginning not a thing is
> Where would the dust alight?

Later, during the Sung dynasty, when several of the famous teachers gathered the Zen teaching devices known as koans into books, the compilers, or later successors, appended gāthās to most of the koans to confirm and extend the thrust of the teaching they embodied. The practice continued into Musō's lifetime. Keizan Jōkin

(1268–1325), a great teacher and a poet who lived earlier in the century during which Musō was born, composed a volume called the *Denkō-roku,* or *Transmission of the Lamp,* a purported compilation of the enlightenment experiences of each of the Patriarchs, from Shākyamuni Buddha to Keizan's Dharma grandfather, Dōgen. Each of the stories was followed, or "capped," by a poem, sometimes though not always a gāthā. And since Keizan was a gifted poet, some of the poems have a clear beauty that does not depend on context.

Musō wrote poems throughout the whole of his adult life, and some are Zen poems in this somewhat ritualized sense. The "Satori Poem" (110) is an example. Some are poems on the deaths of friends, and, like all Musō's poems, they too express their subject from the viewpoint of Zen experience. His poems on the visits and departures of friends, which continue another convention of Chinese poetry, are written in the Zen spirit, as are his most obviously personal poems: the poems of reminiscence and those arising directly from circumstances in his own life, such as the ones about his hut in Miura. These seem to have within their ancestry the poems of the eighth-century Chinese poet Wang Wei, himself a Ch'an (Zen) student during the T'ang dynasty, the golden age of Ch'an.

Since gāthās have usually been translated into English

as quatrains, perhaps it is necessary to explain the form used to translate Musō's gāthās in this collection. The explanation is really my collaborator's, who supplied the first literal versions of these poems in English, with the lines already broken into three sections as they are here. When I asked him why, he wrote to me, "We Japanese Zen priests are expected to learn the traditional chanting of Zen poetry. Even Musō, I think, must have chanted his own poetry just as we do now." He gave several examples, one from a poem of Musō's, the "Satori Poem":

多	年	掘	地	覓	青	天
ta	*nen*	*hotte*	*chi*	*motomu*	*sei*	*ten*
many	year	dig	ground	seek	blue	heaven

which he said would be chanted in Japanese:

Ta-ne-n-n-n
    chio-o-hot-te-e-e
        sei-i-ten-n-n-o-o-o-moto-o-o-mu-u-u-u-u

"In chanting," he said, "a pause matters much, I think.... Truly no translator has ever broken lines. Even D.T. Suzuki didn't. It may be right so far as form is concerned. But I wish to hear Musō's chanting. Unless you feel some awkwardness as English poetry, I myself would like to keep all the poems as they are. If forced to make a choice, I dare to prefer his unheard voices to his written form."

I have since heard the chanting in Shigematsu-san's father's temple, but the broken line, in English, suggested something quite different to me, of course: the breathless rush of Mayakovsky (as it comes across in translation) and above all the delicacy, lightness, and penetrating plainness of the later work of William Carlos Williams. Whatever the original appropriateness of the innovation, I was happy to keep it and to try to make it seem the right form for Musō's poems in English.

As might be guessed from the fact that the translation is a collaboration, I cannot read the original languages: neither the classical Chinese of Musō's poems nor the formal medieval Japanese of his prose. The translation was meant to be as faithful a representation of Musō in English as I could provide with the help of those who could read those languages, but it was not intended for scholars or for those who could read the original. There have been, until now, almost no translations of Musō into English. He is mentioned, of course, in D.T. Suzuki's histories of Zen, but I made my more extensive acquaintance with his work in the biographical and critical writing of Masumi Shibata, and in the French translations Shibata has made with his French wife, Maryse. They have published (Éditions G.P. Maisonneuve et Larose, Paris, 1974) the whole of the *Muchū Mondō* in French, as *Dialogues dans le Rêve*. Soon after I had found that work, conversations with Sōiku Shigematsu led to him sending me, from Japan, the first literal versions of some of Musō's poems, and our collaboration began. We have worked on the versions sporadically over the course of several years, from the first exchange of letters to a theoretically final set of marginal notes that we revised, sitting out the rain under the eaves of the abbot's quarters at Tenryū-ji, looking out at the garden that Musō had designed there, at Hui-neng's Pond, the West Mountains in the mist, the stone waterfall, the stone bridge.

Musō's prose is another venture altogether, and I have included only a few selections that seemed to be particularly helpful in providing a sense of his achievement as a whole. *West Mountain Evening Talk* is a brief collection of his teachings that has been used in Zen monasteries since Musō's death. It and "Musō's Admonition" were given to me in English literal versions prepared by Sōiku. The passages from *Dialogues in the Dream* were translated from the Shibatas' French edition.

His talent apart, Musō's resources as a gardener — the life of his tradition, the dedicated labor — are no longer available. Some of his teaching, like some of the teaching of his great predecessor Dōgen, seems to be almost exclusively relevant to the circumstances of Japanese medieval monasticism. But the vision of existence in gardens and the heart of his teaching seem to me to have survived the transition from one age, one culture — and, in the prose, one language — to another, perhaps not whole, but still, enough so that years of acquaintance with his writing, and what I have seen of his gardens, leave me grateful for what I have glimpsed.

As for the poems, I know only what I have been able to hear from — and, as it were, through — the literals. In such translations, as in all translation, one knows well enough what one was listening for in English, what one would like the translations to be: living poems in the new language, poems that manage to represent the life of the originals. It is too much to hope for, as we all know, and yet one goes on, out of the nature of necessity and of language, trying to put into words that life. Where is it? A poem of Keizan's in the *Denkō-roku* goes something like this:

> The water is clear all the way down.
> Nothing ever polished it. That is the way it is.

W.S.M.
Peahi, Maui, 1989

BIBLIOGRAPHICAL NOTE

Books abound on the history of Buddhism and of Zen. D.T. Suzuki's *Zen and Japanese Culture* (Princeton, Princeton University Press, Bollingen Series, 1957) offers a clear survey.

A number of recent works on Japanese gardens are available in English:

Joseph Conder, *Landscape Gardening in Japan*, New York, Dover, 1964.

Lorraine Kuck, *The World of the Japanese Garden*, New York and Tokyo, Weatherhill, 1968.

Itoh Teiji, *The Japanese Garden: An Approach to Nature*, New Haven, Yale University Press, 1972.

Itoh Teiji, *Space and Illusion in the Japanese Garden*, New York and Tokyo, Weatherhill, 1973.

Mark Holborn, *The Ocean in the Sand*, Boulder, Shambhala, 1978.

For Musō himself, Masumi Shibata's *Les Maîtres du Zen au Japon* (G.P. Maisonneuve et Larose, Paris, 1969) provides a biographical essay, and the introduction to the translation of *Muchū Mondō, Dialogues dans le Rêve* by Masumi and Maryse Shibata (G.P. Maisonneuve et Larose, Paris, 1974), includes, besides the commentary on the dialogues themselves, a discussion of the cultural and historic milieu and the art of gardening that were the context of Musō's work. I have relied extensively on both for my own notes on Musō.

W.S.M.

Sun at Midnight

I

Wandering

A runaway son
    will never own savings
        throughout his life
My treasure
    is the cloud on the peak
        the moon over the valley
Travelling east or west
    light and free
        on the one road
I don't know whether
    I'm on the way
        or at home

2

A Lodging House in Town

Right among the people coming and going
    I have a place to stay
        I shut the gate even in the daytime
and feel as though I had bought
    Wo-chou the great mountain
        and had it with me in town
Never since I was born
    have I liked to argue
        mouth full of blood
My mouth is made fast
    to heaven and earth
        so the universe is still

3

Buddha's Satori

For six years sitting alone
    still as a snake
        in a stalk of bamboo
with no family
    but the ice
        on the snow mountain
Last night
    seeing the empty sky
        fly into pieces
he shook
    the morning star awake
        and kept it in his eyes

4

For Taihei Oshō

I won't let even
    the Buddha and Patriarchs
        through my gate
so I never thought
    to welcome some guests
        and roll my eyes at others
I open the gate a little
    to thank you
        for your visit
and at once the mountains
    and the rivers stand up
        and start the famous dance

5

Rinzan Oshō Visits Me

I leave to the highborn
all the honors
of this dissolving world
A life of poverty
has taught me to love
haze and mist
Today in the spring
the friendship between us
adds warmth to the sunlight
Even a dry post
here on the shore
is blossoming

6

I'm not so deep in it
    as that hermit who held up
        his fist to the guest
but deep enough
    Rinzan Oshō
        for us to be able to talk
Beyond my garden
    the sea begins
        level and boundless
Don't echo Chao-chou's
    "the water's too shallow
        to anchor here"

Reply to Rinzan Oshō

I don't go out
　　to wander around
　　　　I stay home here in Miura
while time flows
　　on through
　　　　the unbounded world
In the awakened eye
　　mountains and rivers
　　　　completely disappear
the eye of delusion
　　looks out upon
　　　　deep fog and clouds
Alone on my zazen mat
　　I forget the days
　　　　as they pass
The wisteria has grown
　　thick over the eaves
　　　　of my hut
The subtle Way
　　of Bodhidharma —
　　　　I never give it a thought

Does anyone know
the truth of Zen
or what to ask about it?

8

Thanks for Daisen Oshō's Visit

Here I have enough to eat
    and I have taken root
        far from the world
People who like to find fault
    can melt even gold with their talk
        why should I listen to that
My mind is weightless
    and without color
        like the lingering fog
The sound of the evening waves
    wakes me
        from my afternoon nap
Cradled in the breast of this mountain
    I have forgotten
        its original wildness
Day after day
    watching the sea
        I have never seen its depths
If I cannot attain
    the very heart
        of Zen

a wave a thousand miles long
will rise up and heave
on the sea beyond my gate

9

Chick feed is what I eat
a quail's nest is where I live
here by the sea
It's all so cramped and huddled
the waves almost touch
the fishermen's huts
It's certainly no place
for entertaining
the rich and famous
and yet a single bubble
contains the whole
limitless sky

Loud thunder
    rattles the mountains
        around this remote village
All at once
    my seclusion my quiet —
        where are they
Don't say that my mouth
    is too small to tell
        of the beauty of the world
In the corner of the garden
    in the winter the plum trees
        are announcing spring

Thanks Sent to Taihei Oshō

I have been lazy
          ever since I was born
                    it would be hard to change now
so I've hidden
          my lump of a body
                    near the edge of the sea
Today Taihei Oshō of Ungan-ji
          surprises me
                    with a visit
I shake his hand
          and we smile
                    in the one wind

From My Hut in Miura

Leaving my footprints
　　nowhere
　　　　south or north
I go into hiding
　　here by the bay full of moonlight
　　　　and the misty hill
I love the life that remains to me
　　here out of sight in the water
　　　　my scales dimmed
I have no wish to leap
　　up the Dragon Gate falls
　　　　to turn into a dragon

13

In these mountain villages and harbor towns
    I'm happy to have found
        good company
a crowd of fishermen
    in and out of my hut
        the whole time
Since I have never held out
    the least thing
        by way of bait
I've managed not to betray
    the fish who have approached
        at the risk of their lives

From the beginning
    the crooked tree
        was no good for a lordly dwelling
How could anyone
    expect the nobles
        to use it for their gates
Now it's been thrown out
    onto the shore
        of this harbor village
handy for the fishermen
    to sit on
        while they're fishing

East of the strait
   beside my hut
      I fish in silence
no more chatter about
   pure land
      impure land
Don't get the idea
   that I'm hoarding salt
      from the black market
I can't cheat the public
   like Tan-hsia
      who dozed on the bridge

My thatched hut
　　the whole sky
　　　　is its roof
the mountains are its hedge
　　and it has the sea
　　　　for a garden
I'm inside
　　with nothing at all
　　　　not even a bag
and yet there are visitors
　　who say "It's hidden
　　　　behind a bamboo door"

All on my own I'm happy
    in the unmapped landscape
        inside the bottle
my only friend
    is this
        wisteria cane
Last night
    we stayed up talking
        so late
that I'm afraid
    I was overheard
        by the empty sky

18

Heaven Peak

Blue blue the summit
    soars above
        fog and cloud
steep and rough
    it stands against
        the empty sky
Everyone who looks up
    gazes in awe
        it seems to go on forever
and each one sees
    the mountains of the earth
        holding it up

19

Gem Mountain

It towers
    from the beginning
        without a flaw
The rain beats upon it
    the wind cuts it
        it only shines brighter
Even fog and cloud
    cannot hide the path
        to the summit
Lin Hsiang-ru was wrong
    running his errand
        to the Ch'in castle

20

Another Summit

It soars alone
    its power stands apart
        from the other mountains
Those who see it
    feel their eyes
        widen
Ever since the boy Sudhana
    was bewildered
        by Meghashri
the blue haze
    the red mist
        have not come to rest

Bamboo Garden

Some crooked some leaning
    bamboos have grown
        by the stone steps of the garden
every year
    there are more of them
        until now they are a forest
At the clack of a stone on a bamboo
    Hsiang-yen shattered
        the uncountable worlds
but this garden
    continues in its green shade
        just as before

To the Emperor's Messenger

The affairs of the world
    are nothing to me
        I am tired of coming and going
This poor hut is perfect for me
    the one possession
        of a monk who does nothing
In the stove
    there is no fire
        and no potato
so I have no time
    to wipe my runny nose and mouth
        to greet the emperor's messenger

23

Old Creek

Since before anyone remembers
    it has been clear
        shining like silver
though the moonlight penetrates it
    and the wind ruffles it
        no trace of either remains
Today I would not dare
    to expound the secret
        of the streambed
but I can tell you
    that the blue dragon
        is coiled there

24

Snow Valley

Each drifting snowflake
　　falls nowhere
　　　　but here and now
Under the settling flowers of ice
　　the water is flowing
　　　　bright and clear
The cold stream
　　splashes out
　　　　the Buddha's words
startling
　　the stone tortoise
　　　　from its sleep

Dry Tree

Leaning all by himself
   on the icy rock
      he has lost all his warmth
His skins have peeled away and body gone
   but still he has not seen
      the wonderland
Now flowers
   have opened
      outside of heaven and earth
and spring winds are blowing there
   nobody knows
      where they are

Old Man in Retirement

I stop worrying about anything
    I give up activities
        I'm full of my life
I no longer
    go to the temple
        evening and morning
If they ask me
    "What are you doing
        in your old age"
I smile and tell them
    "I'm letting my white hair
        fall free"

27

Strange Peak

Looming up forever
    rough and steep —
        what force
The trees look like works of magic
    and all of the stones
        are possessed of powers
Once you climb the peak
    your eyes
        will start from your head
but until then
    it stands veiled in unbroken
        fog and mist

Poem on Dry Mountain (a Zen Garden)

A high mountain
    soars without
        a grain of dust
a waterfall
    plunges without
        a drop of water
Once or twice
    on an evening of moonlight
        in the wind
this man here
    has been happy
        playing the game that suited him

At the Nachi Kannon Hall

The Milky Way
    pours waterfalls
        over this human world
the cold
    rushing tumbling sounds
        echo through the blue sky
Veneration
    to the Great Compassionate
        Avalokiteshvara
How lucky I am
    to have trouble
        hearing

Spring Cliff

Everywhere
    soft breeze warm sunshine
      the same calm
Even the withered trees
    on the dark cliff
      are blossoming
I tried to find
    where Subhūti
      meditates
but suddenly in the shadow
    of mist and fog
      the path splits a thousand ways

Reply to Gen'nō Oshō's Poem

You climb
    Mount Hiei
        on ladders of cloud
I walk
    out of Kyoto
        with a wisteria cane
A thousand miles apart
    like the stars of the east
        and the stars of the north
and this is our one chance
    to remind each other
        that we are friends

For the Death of a Monk

They say that an accident
        is like
                a bellows
but isn't it better
        to go directly
                to the town of Nirvana
Now a spring wind
        is playing for you the tune
                "Return to the Origin"
and even the Buddha's hands
        cannot interfere
                with your homecoming

People's abuse
    has melted what was golden
        and it has gone from the world
Fortune and misfortune
    both belong to the land
        of dreams
Don't look back
    to this world
        your old hole in the cellar
From the beginning
    the flying birds have left
        no footprints on the blue sky

34

To Kengai Oshō of Engaku-ji

Old Man Ho
      once paid the master of the hut
         a surprise visit
Nowhere in the universe
      is it possible to hide
         one's idle everyday life
Yesterday you came
      from Deer's Joy Mountain
         all the way to my hut
and as it happened
      I was not even
         on this mountain

35

Moon Mountain

The light of awakening
     appears when it has been
        forgotten
High and vast the mountain
     lifts forth
        the moon
I myself
     have climbed to
        the summit
In the world outside of things
     there is nothing
        to get in the way

36

Free Old Man

His original way
    is plain and simple
        not caught up in things
He preaches the dharma
    at liquor stores
        and fish shops
He pays no attention
    to sacred rituals
        or secular conventions
Thick white eyebrows
    in his old age
        signs of enlightenment

37

Visiting My Old Hut in Late Spring

At one time I lived
    for several years
        on this beach
now I come
    wandering along here
      as a visitor
The trees around the hut
    still remember me
      and the green
that returns after the flowers
    offers me once more
        what is left of the spring

On the blue waves
    the sun glitters
        the mist is burned away
then the mountains appear
    soaring close to the shore
        each one the most beautiful
Already I have loaded the boat
    to the sinking point
        with the joy of the passing spring
Even Confucius
    who smiled at his disciple's laughter
        would envy what I see

Laughing Mountain

Originally it does not need
        to have Ma-tsu step
            on its foot
Ageless cliff with brushwood grown
        never changing
            from the beginning
It doesn't look high or rugged
        at first nobody sees
            how dangerous it is
But the cloud and mist around it
        hide a forest
            of swords

Inauguration of Fukusan Dormitory

Sacred and secular
    originally live
        in the same house
With compassionate hands
    the Great Master has opened
        the gate for the first time
Don't ask who
    or how many
        are in the hall
These tiles and rafters
    cover all
        of heaven and earth

41

Cloud Mountain

Living secluded
    above the cloud
        at the top of Mount Sū
abiding in your origin
    you demonstrate
        the truth of Zen
The sharp sword of wisdom
    raised between your eyebrows
        rests in your palms
You have moved far from town
    from now on you renew
        the Way of Bodhidharma

At Gen's Embarkation for Yuan China

Deep grief wringing the heart
    promising over and over to meet again
        you leave Deer's Joy Mountain
The colors of spring
    in a hundred castle gardens
        all live in your staff
After you have known
    the great death
        once and for all
may the original sail
    bring you east
        again to this land

At Kan's Embarkation for Yuan China

Setting out over the sea to the south
    looking for the truth —
        but it's too late
Sailing all that way
    what do you hope to find
        over the ocean
Right here and now
    I'll spare you thirty blows
        for a while
and wait for you to come back
    some day
        in brocade robes

44

At Iku's Embarkation for Yuan China

Whale billows
    thousands of miles
        all the way to the end of the sky
don't betray
    the boundless clear wind
        and the bright moon
When you have
    worn out
        your straw sandals
you will be back
    leaping free
        of the pit of Nang-yang

45

Mourning for the Layman Named Cloud Peak

In your old age
    giving up your career you lived
        free of the concerns of the world
You gave no more thought
    to your own achievements
        that had cost you such sweat
In the hollow night
    the ship sails on
        but where is it going
Age after age
    you will raise a green peak
        through the clouds

46

Patriarch Peaks

Twenty-eight Indian Patriarchs
    six Chinese all reveal
        the subtle working of Zen
Higher and higher
    they soar into the blue sky
        dwarfing the five summits of Mount Sumeru
Naturally their successors
    come and try
        to climb their peaks
The dharma that has reached
    its golden summit
        never falls away

47

East Peak

From the beginning
    people have gazed in awe at Taigaku
        the East Peak
It shoots up into the heavens
    on it the sun rises
        the moon rises
Its original blue and yellow
    are not among the colors
        of other mountains
It will hold the spring sunlight
    year after year
        after year

48

Old Hut

A handful of thatch
    has sheltered its master's head
        since before time began
Now some new students
    are gathering to wait
        outside the gate
Don't say
    there's nothing
        new at all
Year after year
    in this garden
        the trees blossom

49

Tengan Oshō's Visit to Erin-ji

With your tall
        golden staff tinkling
                you have come all the way down
Talking for days
        about things not of the world
                our words have been all we needed
Sumptuous the colors
        of the halls
                and the temple buildings
Lush and dense around them
        the serene beauty of the forest
                and the arbored walks
Lovely! Our hearts are open
        Not a grain of sand
                in our friendship
May it go on just like this!
        In the floating world of things
                needles hide in the carpet
The memory of this visit
        should be handed down
                forever

There is something beyond happiness
inside the gate
of this mountain

Living in the Mountains:
Ten Poems

In this small hut
    are worlds beyond number
Living here alone
    I have endless company
Already I have
    attained the essence
How could I dare
    to want something higher?

Among rocks and valleys
    deep in the folds of this mountain
the dharma does not go
    up or down
Having seen through
    Huang-lung's mind
I plant vegetables
    around my meditation seat

Very high this mountain
    and few find their way up here
Only puffs of cloud
    drift up and past
As I meditate my Original Self
    empties all of heaven and earth
like the lantern
    in broad day

All worries and troubles
     have gone from my breast
and I play joyfully
     far from the world
For a person of Zen
     no limits exist
The blue sky must feel
     ashamed to be so small

A curtain of cloud hangs
    before the meditation seat
an ice wheel of moonlight
    turns through the railing
Don't say I have erased
    all trace of attainment
Behind me there are still
    heaven and earth

Don't ask suspiciously
        why I have shut the gate
                and remain alone
Hiding light
        is the way
                one gives light
Thunder roars and roars
        but nobody
                hears it
On the other hand people say
        that the valley is so deep
                the dragon comes out late

I wake from my noon nap
    and see the shadows
        moving in the afternoon
Mist fades from the old cedar
    and I am face to face
        with Haku Mountain
Thirty years
    so many events
        have come and gone
Now I let them all go
    and sit in the stillness
        and am still

Green mountains
    have turned yellow
        so many times
the troubles and worries
    of the world of things
        no longer bother me
One grain of dust in the eye
    will render the Three Worlds
        too small to see
When the mind is still
    the floor where I sit
        is endless space

Time for a walk
in the world outside
and a look at who I am
Originally I had no cares
and I am seeking
nothing special
Even for my guests
I have nothing
to offer
Except these white stones
and this clear
springwater

With compassionate hands
    Buddha and Patriarchs
        constantly save those who are lost
Crimes and errors
    fill the whole sky
        and who knows it
Is there anything better
    than to stay at the foot
        of this misty cliff
watching in meditation
    the calm clouds
        on their way home to the cave?

60

Pine Shade

A hedge
>of a thousand trees
>>standing in the cold
The green haze
>so deep and dense
>>it keeps out the light
Don't blame me
>for staying alone
>>with my door shut
The guidepost
>always has been open
>>for anyone who comes

61

Plum Window

The flowers on one tree have opened
    and six houses
        are full of the sweet scent
I have managed to transmit
    the Sixth Patriarch's
        fragrant teaching
Now all the counties
    are made happy
        by the coming of spring
What monkey
    still hangs back
        in dreamland

Jewel Field

I have cultivated
    a piece of overgrown
        wasteland
All the soil now
    is beginning
        to shed light
Autumn
    is the time
        of harvest
Each grain gathered
    is worth
        several castles

Truth Hall

First the outer gate
    then the inner gate
        under the high roof the low roof
Deep within
    there is no argument
        to be heard
Each of you be sure
    to find the deepest truth
        in yourself
and say "Maitreya
    Buddha of the future
        plenty, thank you!"

64

No Precedent

Beyond any
    link with the world
        he really is
To him the Buddha's and Patriarchs'
    preachings are
        wasted breath
He has gone now
    leaving behind nothing
        nothing at all
The great roc
    will never rest
        in the green paulownia branches

Old Man To-The-Point

No inheritance
    is like that from a true
        heir of the dharma
and there is no other school
    or different sect
        with which to quarrel
In your old age
    you have gone deeper
        into the truth under everything
and your eyebrows
    one-foot-two-inch-long
        have grown from your chin

66

Old Man Advancing

Beyond the point where the rivers
    end and the mountains vanish
        you have kept on walking
Originally
    the treasure lies
        just under one's feet
You made the mistake of thinking
    that now you would be able
        to retire in peace
Look: in your own hut
    the meditation mat
        has never been warm

Abiding Mountain

A violent storm
        beats against it
                but it never moves at all
Wild and solitary
        sharp and full of power
                it soars like a bird's feather
I give my assent only
        to one who has climbed
                to the summit
Walking sitting lying down
        he does everything as though
                he were out for a stroll

68

Snow Garden

Flowers with six petals
    have covered the whole ground
        and frozen everywhere
Heaven and earth have disappeared
    into this one
        pure color
A pine and a cedar
    by the stone stairs
        are still green
Shen-kuan
    must have lost sight of the mind
        of the great vessel

69

One Hut

The endless worlds
        have all gathered
                in this small hut
In the four directions
        and above and below
                there is no neighbor
All living beings
        secular and sacred
                live in here
Old Man Ho
        why do you go off visiting
                somebody else?

Moon Tree Cliff

The moon trees keep growing and growing
    their blossoms sweep
        the wide ribbon of cloud
No one
    has ever climbed the high branches
        hidden in leaves
Subhūti has sat in his cave
    for years on end
        with his mind far away
not knowing that he is
    in the moon tree cave
        on the moon

Gem Creek

The mysterious valley fountain
　　is originally bright and clear
　　　　it was not made by humans
The banks on both sides
　　and the stream between them
　　　　all shine with one light
Without ruffling the surface
　　look carefully
　　　　into the depths
You'll see the uncountable
　　legendary jewels
　　　　of the Kunlun Mountains

No-Word Hut

I left my locked mouth
    hanging
        on the wall
With the brushwood
    door shut tight
        I delight in my own freedom
Inside
    my secret talk resounds
        like thunder
Even the bare
    posts and the lamps
        can't pretend they don't hear it

Old Mountain

Out of the green of spring
    and the yellow of autumn
        all by yourself you went
into the numberless mountains
    and you have stayed there
        hidden for many years
Even the clouds
    shun those peaks
        nothing obstructs the view
The eternal landscape
    of no season
        is spread before you

No End Point

The whole world is clear and empty
        to the ten directions
            There is no end point
And yet when we
        look carefully
            there is one after all
You fly out of this world
        looking backward
            riding the giant roc
into the hollow of a lotus thread
        to live there where heaven and earth
            were never divided

Lover of Mountains

Your compassionate mind
        soars like a summit
                there is your true effortless nature
some places smooth and gentle
        some places rugged and
                unapproachable
The mountain has
        no wish to be
                looked up to
It is only people
        who look up
                in wonder

Sūzan Oshō's Visit

Mountains on all sides
     rivers looped around it
          there's no trail to my hut
When the dragon-elephant approaches
     a path opens
          all by itself
In the hour of soaring talk
     neither has to think
          of meeting the other halfway
though all of you
     keep wandering into
          yes and no

Reply to Sūzan Oshō's Snow Poem

In one night
>ice flowers have filled
>>all the forests and streams
There shining clearly
>is Bodhidharma's guidepost
>>a thousand years old
Inside the one color
>there is no
>>stir of Zen
Shen-kuan stands in vain
>in snow
>>up to his waist

The Pure Sound Gate of the Riverside Temple

The monastery
    like the moon in the water —
        heaven and earth are wide
The gate is reflected
    a hundred pavilions
        a thousand
A complete existence
    nothing missing nothing left over
        no need for the water to wash the ears clear
Day and night
    outside the gate
        the wide river flows

For Gen the New Head Priest of Erin-ji

Not leaving your
      Zen practice behind
           in the dreams of the Heavenly Palace
all by yourself
      you realize the elegance
         beyond elegance
Your old staff tinkling
      in the chilling dew and frost
         pierces heaven
In the Temple of the Forest of Wisdom
      the fruit is ripe
         now is the time

80

For Myō's Departure for Anzen-ji

Now the splendor of the Patriarch's Garden
    is smudged with the rising
        dust of war
Everywhere
    Zen students are sitting
        on mats of needles
No doubt your visit
    will bring good fortune
        upon the Temple of the Joy of Zen
The chill wind of wisdom
    from one tinkling staff
        is worth words beyond number

For Myō's Departure for Shōfuku-ji

A single true man
　　appears in the world
　　　　and all falsehood vanishes
No need to worry
　　that the Way of the Patriarchs
　　　　seems to be declining
This time
　　your ax of wisdom
　　　　has found wings
Some day
　　surely it will rise up
　　　　and fly

For Tetsu the New Head Priest of Erin-ji

For a long time
the world
has been decaying
The Way of the Patriarchs
declines day by day
nothing to do about it
Good! Now the one monk
whose hands are never
tucked in his sleeves
enters
the Forest of Wisdom
with his ax held high

83

For Shō the New Head Priest of Erin-ji

Actions to save the world
    have their ups and downs
        depending on circumstances
You have to be as careful
    as though you were dragging half a ton
        by a hair
Spare no efforts
    to bring the dharma rain
        to this countryside
The Forest of Wisdom
    will grow dense
        and cover the whole world

84

At Whole-World-In-View Hut

The heavens allowed me
  to settle myself
    on a small piece of land
Looking into the distance
  digging far down
    I delight in my own freedom
All who come here
  feel the lids fall
    from their eyes
This view
  of the world without end—
    there is nowhere to hide

85

Ashikaga Tadayoshi's Palace

When the blind is raised
    at the clear window
        one is facing the East Mountains
The magnificent landscape
    stretches away
        from the edge of the table
Everyone feels the silk veil
    drawn back
        from before his face
Illusions carried
    through many lives
        vanish in one moment

86

Climbing Down the Snowy Mountain

From inside the room
        you can't tell whether it's snowing
                outside or not
Don't judge
        Zen students
                sorting them into three piles
Sometimes one of them
        will bolt suddenly
                out to the endless mountains
kick over a peak
        and grind it
                underfoot

87

Snow at Rōhatsu Sesshin

I have slept by the cold window
    and come back
        from the land of dreams
The eye of my mind
    has opened by itself
        with no need of the morning star
All of heaven and earth
    hold up this mountain
        covered with snow
Where in the world
    is there a place
        for Shākyamuni to practice?

88

It

One by one many leaves
    the colors of autumn
        let go of their twigs and fall
The cold cloud full of rain
    passes above
        the hollow of the mountain
Everyone alive
    is born gifted
        with true sight
How do you see
    these koans
        with your own eyes?

89

Magnificent Peak

By its own nature
    it towers above
        the tangle of mountains
Don't say
    it's a lot of dirt
        piled high
Without end the mist of dawn
    the evening cloud
        draw their shadows across it
From the four directions
    you can look up and see it
        green and steep and wild

Reply to Bukkō Zenji's Poem at Seiken-ji

I remember that once
  my dharma grandfather
    was happy to visit here
I feel ashamed sometimes
  to be inferior still
    to the seagull he saw then
But I'm lucky
  to hold in one phrase
    all the words of all the ages
Above the channel
  the full moon
    is shining on the shore

Snow

Flowers of ice
    hide the heavens
        no more blue sky
a silver dust
    buries all the fields
        and sinks the green mountains
Once the sun
    comes out on the one
        mountaintop
even the cold
    that pierces to the bone
        is a joy

92

Gem Forest

Long shadows
   woven with light
      dispel all trees but these
Even the bead trees of Japan
   even gardenias
      are not worth admitting
Polished by wind
   buffed by rain
      a forest without a flaw
each leaf
   each branch
      a treasure alone of its kind

93

Withered Zen

Both sacred wisdom
 and ordinary feeling
  have completely fallen away
No craving
 for success and fame
  rises in my mind
Don't tell me that I've
 fallen into
  a frosty stone cave
Inside my heart
 I keep three thousand
  prancing chestnut horses

94

The Fragrance of the Udumbara

Once in a thousand years
    the Udumbara blooms
        It has opened its auspicious flowers
Many labored
    to bring it
        from India to Japan
Its heady fragrance
    lingers
        without fading
and is not lost
    among the thousand grasses
        the countless weeds

95

House of Spring

Hundreds of open flowers
    all come from
        the one branch
Look
    all their colors
        appear in my garden
I open the clattering gate
    and in the wind
        I see
the spring sunlight
    already it has reached
        worlds without number

96

No Gain

Virtue and compassion
    together make up
        each one's integrity
Nothing that comes through the gate
    from outside
        can be the family treasure
Throwing away
    the whole pile
        in your heart
with empty hands
    you come
        bringing salvation

97

Seashore

Stretching into the distance
    the sea
        swallows a hundred rivers
for thousands of miles
    the spray joins the waves
        to the sky
What is true
    of the time you put up
        the old sail
Right there
    you come to know
        where it is

98

For Ko Who Has Come Back from China

A brief meeting today
     but it seems to gather up
       a hundred years
We have exchanged
     the compliments of the season
       that's word-of-mouth Zen
Don't say that
     ignorance and wisdom
       belong to opposing worlds
Look: China and Japan
     but there are not
       two skies

*Ten Scenes in the
Dragon of Heaven Temple*

99

The Gate of Universal Light

The great light of compassion
    illuminates this world
        in every part
As a boy
    Sudhana stood
        before the gates
when his eyes
    closed over the whole
        empty world
But at the snap of Maitreya's finger
    the gate has opened
        just like that

Incomparable-Verse Valley

The sounds of the stream
    splash out
        the Buddha's sermon
Don't say
    that the deepest meaning
        comes only from one's mouth
Day and night
    eighty thousand poems
        arise one after the other
and in fact
    not a single word
        has ever been spoken

Hall of the Guardian God

Inside the temple enclosure
    a place was set aside
        for a Shinto shrine
Wish with your whole self
    for the divine wind
        to help the Way of the Patriarchs
Don't ask why the pine trees
    in the front garden
        are gnarled and crooked
The straightness
    they were born with
        is right there inside them

Hui-neng's Pond

The dharma spring of the Sixth Patriarch
    has never run dry
        it is flowing even now
a single drop
    has fallen and spread
        far and deep
Don't be caught
    by the decorations at the edge
        and the bank around it
In the dead of night
    the moonlight strikes
        the middle of the pond

The Peak of the Held-Up Flower

On Vulture Peak
    once the Buddha
        held up a flower
It has been multiplied
    into a thousand plants
        One of them is on this mountain
Look: the fragrant seedlings
    have been handed all the way down
        to the present
No one knows
    how many spring winds are blowing
        in the timeless world

104

The Bridge Where the Moon Crosses

It arches like a rainbow
    dividing the stream
        joining the shores
one line
    a road bringing life
        crosses the quiet waves
It has carried
    donkeys across horses across
        but there is more to come
In the middle of the night
    the moon is crossing it
        pushing a cart

Three-Step Waterfall

At dangerous places
　　awesome ledges
　　　　three barriers
The loud water rushes
　　The spray of the fall hovers
　　　　It's hard to find the way
So many fish
　　have fallen back
　　　　with the stamp of failure on their foreheads
Who knows that this
　　wind of blood
　　　　is lashing the whole universe?

Cave of the Thousand Pines

One heaven and earth
    deep in
        ten thousand pines
Green haze
    flickering
        hides the mouth of the cave
The heaven of a hermit
    belongs originally
        to a hermit
Don't say
    this place is not
        the earthly heaven

Dragon-Gate House

With no help
    from the Giant Spirit's
        mountain-shattering fist
the two peaks allowed
    a wide river
        to flow between them
Late at night
    no one
        is coming
Beyond the railing
    of the hut
        a few puffs of passing cloud

108

Turtle Head Stupa

A pine tree
 with long needles
  has grown behind it
On top of the tower
 there is a Buddha image
  of eternal happiness
Now the doors and windows
 are all open
  and nothing inside is hidden
Dharma worlds
 beyond number
  are there for you to see

◆◆◆

Tiger Valley

Steep mountains
    deep valley
        no one finds the way there
Tigers gather
    and fight
        fiercely together
The three saints
    crossing the bridge
        hand in hand
have mistaken the sound
    of the water
        for laughter

Tōki-no-Ge (Satori Poem)

Year after year
    I dug in the earth
        looking for the blue of heaven
only to feel
    the pile of dirt
        choking me
until once in the dead of night
    I tripped on a broken brick
        and kicked it into the air
and saw that without a thought
    I had smashed the bones
        of the empty sky

III

The Garden at the General's Residence

The beautiful landscape
> of the three famous god-mountains
>> has all been reproduced here
Rough standing stones
> a stream meandering
>> delight without end
How lovely! The setting
> for elegant play
>> and serene pleasure
No doubt the dharma stream
> from the Sixth Patriarch's valley
>> runs through here

112

Temple of Eternal Light

The mountain range
    the stones in the water
        all are strange and rare
The beautiful landscape
    as we know
        belongs to those who are like it
The upper worlds
    the lower worlds
        originally are one thing
There is not a bit of dust
    there is only this still and full
        perfect ornament

Mugoku Oshō's Snow Poem

Everyone sees
 only the falling
  scentless flowers
No one has yet understood
 where the flakes fly
  and where they fall
Now you excellent monk
 are sitting
  in the meditation hall
You know that the mind
 rises from the origin
  in the eighth consciousness, doesn't it?

114

Sūzan Oshō's Visit to My West Mountain Hut

A few puffs of white cloud
    drift around the mouth
      of the valley
without hindering
    my dharma friend when he comes
      to knock at my door
I've never found a way
    to hide my doing nothing
      day after day
We join hands
    and walk back and forth
      back and forth

On the Wall of Cloud-Friend Hut

The cliff
  towers beside the cave
    shutting out the light
Half the space
  in the six-foot bamboo hut
    is given over to cloud
Living alone
  a person takes
    pleasure in such things
not regretting
  the absence
    of swarming visitors

Digging Out the Buddha Relic

From under the ground
       it emerges into the world
             offering enlightenment
The small circle of light
       spreading around it
             holds the numberless worlds
It is hard
       to measure and weigh
             its rarity
Clear and light unmistakably
       there it lies
             by the hoe

Reply to a Friend's Poem

Our karma led
    you and me
        to live on separate mountains
It is hard to speak
    as the wind does
        across a thousand miles
But nothing comes between
    the cloud in Ch'u
        and the water in Yueh
Meeting in our old age
    we are happy to talk
        day and night

Ox Turned Loose

Ignoring lash and rope
    he moves along following
        the Original Nature
He is playing outside the fence
    he won't look back
        at anyone
There is no way
    that I could have found
        his tracks anywhere
but look he shows his whole body
    in worlds
        countless as dust and sand

Clear Valley

The water that can't be muddied
    with any stick
        is deeper than depth
The sky and the water
    are a single
        deepening blue
If you really want to find
    the source of the Sixth Patriarch's
        fountain
don't look for it
    on the one bank or on the other
        or in the middle of the stream

Old Man at Leisure

Sacred or secular
    manners and conventions
        make no difference to him
Completely free
    leaving it all to heaven
        he seems like a simpleton
No one catches
    a glimpse inside
        his mind
this old man
    all by himself
        between heaven and earth

Ancient Origin

One drop of dharma water
    from the Sixth Patriarch's valley
        was there before the first legendary Buddha
It comes from a great distance
    and I know that its source
        is far within
Pity the one who has not yet
    come home
        from over the sea
and goes on looking somewhere else
    for the great subtle mind
        of the Buddha of India

Old Man of Few Words

The silent old man
    asked me to write
        a poem for him
The silly contradictions
    in the one I composed
        made people laugh to death
Look carefully again
    at the truth
        of nonduality
then even Vimalakīrti's
    jaw will drop
        like bark from a birch tree

123

Jewel Cliff

Sharp facets
    a brightness
        not made by cutting
Eight faces
    clear and bright
        no stain anywhere
Good! Here is
    the very form
        of transcendent wisdom
Day and night
    all the gods in heaven
        will rain flowers upon it

Joy Mountain

Grasses and trees
    look different
        and the auspices are good
Puffs of cloud
    delight in trailing
        around the peak
A thousand mountains
    a million hills
        look up to its virtue
Is there anyone
    who has never been blessed
        with its shelter

125

For a Monk Going West

For many years
    our friendship
        has ripened
One morning
    you say goodbye
        and start down to the west
Stop trying to find the secret
    of succeeding
        as head priest
Look the sharp ax
    has been in your hands
        since the beginning

Flat Mountain

Broad and flat
 it emerges
   beyond height
Seven shoulders
  eight hollows
   all shelve to one plane
No one
  knows where
   the summit is
From the beginning
  there was never
   a path to it

Beyond the World

This place of wild land
    has no boundaries
        north south east or west
It is hard to see
    even the tree
        in the middle of it
Turning your head
    you can look beyond
        each direction
For the first time
    you know that your eyes
        have been deceiving you

128

Beyond Light

The clear mirror
        and its stand
                have been broken
There is no dust
        in the eyes
                of the blind donkey
Dark
        dark everywhere
                the appearance of subtle Zen
Let it be
        The garden lantern
                opens its mouth laughing

Hut in Harmony

When the master
    without a word
        raises his eyebrows
the posts and rafters
    the cross-beams and roof-tree
        begin to smile
There is another place
    for conversing
        heart to heart
The full moon
    and the breeze
        at the half-open window

130

Lamenting the Civil War

So many times since antiquity
    the human world
        has barely escaped destruction
yet ten thousand fortunes
    and a thousand misfortunes
        end in one void after all
Puppets squabbling
    back and forth
        across the stage
People brawling
    over a snail's horn
        winning or losing
The ferocity
    of a snipe and a clam
        glaring at each other
only to arrive after death
    before the tribunal
        of Yama the Judge of Hell
When will the horses of war
    be turned loose
        on Flower Mountain

It would be best
        to throw their bits away
                to the east of the Buddha's Palace

Letters

West Mountain Evening Talk

When the Master was living at Nanzen-ji as a head priest, Gen'nō Oshō said to him, "For the last twenty years, ever since you finished your study in the monasteries, you have been moving from one place to another. By now you have changed the place you live more than ten times. I think this is harmful to a Zen student. It exhausts him and interferes with his practice. But recently I read the *Sutra for the Period of the Imitative Dharma* and according to that, the Buddha said, 'Students must stay at one place for no more than three months. Anyone who accuses those who move on of being flighty will go to Hell.' That disposed of some of my concern."

The Master answered, "It was not because of the Buddha's words that I kept moving on. I think of his enlightenment as my home, and I never left that whether I went off to the east or stayed behind in the west. Some people stay at one monastery for a long time but they do not always sit on the same Zen mat. Sometimes they leave it to wash their hands or faces. Sometimes they walk in the garden or climb a mountain to look out over the country. You might say that they too were rather frivolous.

But because their minds are fixed on the one point even when they are moving around it is not correct to say that they are somewhere else. If they can free their limited minds and play in the boundless world, there is nothing to reproach them for, is there?"

A monk said to the Master, "You are a descendant of Lin-chi [in Japanese, Rinzai] Zenji, but you do not teach your students in the traditional Rinzai way. Instead you always give lectures on the sutras. Why is that?"

The Master answered, "For a Zen student, knowledge-understanding and practice-understanding must go together. Even then the student will not be able to benefit everyone until he has found the right person and the right circumstances. I am still no more than a fledgling, and my ability is only partly formed. I have not met the one teacher or found the best circumstances. So it is a mistake to be too critical of me.

"Nowadays there is a tendency among Zen followers who cannot see into themselves or into the subtle workings of Zen to memorize old saws just to keep a dialogue turning like a wheel, and sometimes they push or pull in some manner that's supposed to look like Zen. They flatter themselves that in doing things like that they are manifesting the heart of the dharma. None of that amounts to anything. They're deceiving themselves. It's not hard to imitate the manners of the ancients, but it's very difficult to attain their virtue. I don't think much of those who set such store by externals and never notice their own lack of virtue."

The monk went on, "Then why do you preside over a *sangha*, comment on the sayings of our predecessors, and expound the sutras?"

The Master replied, "Those who do evil do it not because they want to go to hell but because of an earlier karma. I myself would not dare to aspire to the title of 'master.' Just the same I lead a *sangha* only because some remnant of virtue enacted in a former life impels me to do it. I don't wish to enjoy a retired life with my gate shut. And it follows, just as my arms swing when I walk, that I expound the sutras, comment on the words of the Patriarchs, and in that way allow those who do not believe in the law of cause and effect to learn that it exists, and help people who know nothing of Mahayana and of Zen to learn the truth. Once a Zen master served tea to travellers beside the road for the purpose of sharing the dharma with many people. My purpose is the same when I talk about the sayings and teaching of the Buddha and the Patriarchs."

The monk asked, "Many priests and laypeople

nowadays believe in Zen, so why do you say that you have not had a chance to meet someone suited to you?"

The Master answered, "I don't mean that no one has Zen insight, but only that no one's view accords completely with mine."

The monk went on, "Even a dull student, though he may not attain satori, will grasp something of the dharma if you show it to him directly. Why do you ignore someone like that?"

The Master answered, "Haven't you heard the saying, 'A thousand-pound bow and arrow won't hit a mouse'? The Buddha came to this world and his silent words and his long sermons have filled the sutra storehouse to overflowing. Why didn't he simply show the truth? You should consider that. Yuan-wu says, 'First deprive students of their preconceptions, and then they will be ready to undergo the ordinary rigorous Zen practice.' And Ta-hui says, 'Zen teachers should preach dharma only according to their students' levels of Zen understanding. The master's way of teaching, sudden as a flint spark or a flash of lightning, can be grasped only by those who are ready for it. To use Zen methods of that kind with novices would be like pulling up young shoots that have just been planted out.'"

The monk continued, "Are you saying that the Buddha's teachings really are not true?"

The Master replied, "All of your questions miss the point. So the answers I've been giving you can't be worth much either. I have made mud pies of words just to try to help you understand. A man once wrote to Yuan-wu, 'Please give me a koan.' Yuan-wu answered, 'I hear you have always read the *Sutra on Perfect Enlightenment*. My koan for you is in that.'

"Yuan-wu usually gave his students koans such as 'Mount Sumeru,' 'The Dry Shit-Stick,' and 'Chao-chou's Mu.' What kind of koan is 'Read the Sutra'? But if you understand what Yuan-wu really meant, you will see that not only the *Sutra on Perfect Enlightenment* but the other thousand sutras and ten thousand sayings, and even secular gossip and idle chatter, all of them without exception, are precisely the koans of the Patriarchs and the teachings of the Buddha. How dare you say that this is not true? Do you still criticize me for lecturing on the sutras and insist that I am not competent to be a Zen teacher?

"Once a master said, 'Before the days of Ma-tsu and Pai-chang teachers put much emphasis on *richi* [intellectual learning] and little on *kikan* [Zen practice].' What did he really mean? That the earlier teachers displayed nothing but intellectual understanding because they were without true insight? Or that those of later times lacked insight and so guided their students from the point of view of practice only, contradicting their predecessors? The teachings of the Patriarchs, as you know, are very different from the elucidations of Buddhist scholars, who never get further than 'one foot is one foot and two feet are two feet.' To be able to make one's actions really accord with circumstances, watching the movements of the opponent and breaking through them, this is the meaning of the well-known Zen phrase, 'family broken up, house ruined.' Today people divide up into two groups, those who believe in practice and those who put their trust in intellectual understanding, but neither of them has got out of the scholars' gate. The Buddha said, 'From my first sermon at the Deer Park to my last one by the Hiranyavati River I have not preached a single word.' If you can see what he meant by that you may praise me or abuse me as you please."

The Master used to say to us when we were his students, "When I was twenty I became a novice at Ken'nin-ji. I never left the zendō at all but gave myself up completely to my practice. The next winter I went down east to enroll at the zendō of Kenchō-ji. An old priest there gave me this advice: 'The records of the phrases and sayings that have been saved from the satori experiences of the Zen masters of the past have been written down only in order to help Zen students to reach satori through the contemplation of those words. But many people today trade secondhand Zen stories, gossip, rumors, and they use the collections any way they please. And there are people besides who call themselves Zen monks but do zazen in an absentminded way, without bothering to learn from the great teachers or read the records of the Patriarchs. All of them are ignorant of why those books were preserved for us. In this degenerate latter day of the dharma it is very hard to find true teachers. But if we read the records in order to encourage our own earnest aspiration, we will come to see that the forerunners' satori experiences are really our own, here and now. Where in the world, then, is the difference between past and present?'

"I followed his advice and in the hours outside zazen time, back in the sleeping hall, I read the records. At that time Issan Kokushi was in charge of both Kenchō-ji and Engaku-ji. For some years I became his disciple. From morning till evening I learned directly from his teachings and from the Zen of the Five Schools. I began to flatter myself that I had grasped the whole truth of Zen Buddhism. But when I looked back into my own mind I found the same old uncertainty there. It had never changed. Finally I realized that 'nothing that is brought through the gate from the outside is the real family treasure.' A master once said, 'The light of the spirit must always be clear. That is the unalterable rule. Once you have entered the gate of Zen, do not put your faith in intellectual understanding.' I had left Buddhist theory only to lose myself in Zen scholarship. The two kinds of study may appear to be different, but both of them are based on intellectual understanding. If I had gone on that way I would have dimmed the light of my own spirit. So I gathered up all the odds and ends that I had treasured up until then and put them in my satchel, and without a moment's hesitation threw them into the fire.

"As it happened, Bukkoku Zenji was then in charge of Manju-ji. I entered his room for the first time and told him what I was trying to find. Bukkoku sighed and said, 'When I was sixteen I became a Zen student at Tōfuku-ji, under the guidance of an old priest. He told me to read the Zen classics. Each line that I read I asked him about, and he said to me, "The words that are used in Zen are different from those of the other sects of Buddhist doctrine, and I would not dare to say anything about them." I went on, "But how can we understand what they mean if there is no explanation?" He said to me, "Satori is something you must arrive at without help from anyone." I said, "If I try very hard to understand the Zen classics, will that lead me to satori?" He answered, "If you really want to attain satori you should do your best without relying on books." As soon as I heard that I stopped reading, and instead I devoted myself entirely to zazen, back in the zendō. Several of my friends came and kept advising me: "While you are young you must study, first of all. Your momentary zeal for the dharma cannot be expected to last. In your old age you will surely regret what you are doing." But my mind was firmly made up, and I continued my zazen harder than ever. Now I am over sixty years old but I have nothing to regret.' My teacher laughed as he said it.

"Once he had given me his advice I made up my mind to do the best I could. I practiced zazen every day whatever the weather. My practice did seem to advance a little, but I did not arrive at any final breakthrough. So I decided to look for a retreat deep in the mountains and try to see my Original Self. I left Engaku-ji and went to the Deep North to build a hut far out in the mountains. I made a vow to myself. I said, 'I will either come to see my Original Self clearly or I will die among the grass and trees.' As a *keisaku* [warning stick] I kept three books on my table, Yuan-wu's *Essential Principles of Mind*, Ta-hui's *Letters*, and Chueh-fan's *Forest Life*, but no other possessions. I spent three years in my secluded life in the mountains, but I had not yet reached a final view. One day I remembered Bukkoku Zenji's parting words: 'If a Zen student makes the slightest distinction between the secular world and priestly world, satori will remain unattainable.' I realized that although I had coveted nothing at all in this secular world, my desire for the dharma had ensnared my mind and stood in the way of enlightenment. When I realized what my mistake had been, even my craving vanished, and from then on I could spend every day with my mind empty. And one night I happened to kick over the nests and dens of delusion that I had kept clinging to, and at last I saw that Bukkoku's words are true.

"So I gave those three books that I had treasured to my friends. I stayed away from books, and never let my back or my sides rest on the bed. In that way I spent twenty years doing nothing special. But as I grow older my body is growing weaker, and now it is a little hard for me to sit zazen for very long at a time. The winds of karma have led me to preside over a few temples and to teach students, and to run back and forth, east and west. My daily life is not what I wanted at the beginning, but I have not clouded over my own original light, even in the dusty world, and that was because I had practiced zazen as hard as I could, sitting persistently and not sleeping in bed. My teachings and sermons in the dharma hall, my talks on the records of the Patriarchs, and my lectures on the sutras in response to people's questions may sound a little unusual, but I am not concerned about that. That is all because of my turning away from intellectual interpretation years ago. Now I have come to understand what a Zen master meant when he said, 'The more is hidden, the more appears.' Hide it, and hide it, and hide it! When there is nothing more to hide, the original, inborn 'great function and great working' appears all by itself. Never, never doubt that."

The Master said, "Bukkō Zenji's advice to his disciple Bukkoku goes:

> I doubt that many students in Japan will attain satori in their lifetimes. Some students in this country tend to admire intellectual understanding instead of trying to attain satori. It is a pity that students with great capacity waste their whole lives reading widely in the native and foreign classics, cultivating the art of composition, and in that way leaving no time for coming to see clearly into their Original Nature. There are students of another kind who do not have this wide knowledge and culture, but think it best to sit in zazen absentmindedly, never making any real effort to seek the Way. People like this will never reach satori, either, however long they remain in the world.

"When my teacher, Bukkoku, told me this, I said, 'Apart from those who are born with the capacity for immediately perceiving the truth, which of the two you have described is superior?' My teacher answered, 'Even students with little ability can attain satori in this life. If they continue diligently in their zazen until the last day of the last year of their lives, a single word will be enough for them to attain satori a thousand times over. On the other hand, those who rely on their learning will not only waste their lives in this world, but in their next lives too they will fall into a world that they would rather avoid.'"

A monk said to the Master, "Those who use their scholarship to seem superior to others are beyond consideration. But why do you criticize those Zen students who have studied the Zen classics and so give off the light of wisdom?"

The Master answered, "Second-rate and third-rate students cannot go back at once to their own Original Home. So out of pity for them the Patriarchs built temporary inns for them, which are like the classics you mention. In a sense these inns are good to have. Everyone needs sermons on the sutras at the sutra inns, sermons on the precepts at the precept inns, commentary on the records of Zen at the commentary inns. So there is no reason to rule out Zen preaching entirely.

"But a priest once said, 'Bodhidharma came to China from India. And without relying on words and letters he pointed straight at the mind and brought students to realize satori.' And he went on, 'If looking into the true self is merely a matter of words, the whole of Buddhist scripture is nothing but words. Then what is the meaning of Bodhidharma's coming to China?' Huang-po says, 'If any of you students wishes to be a Buddha, there is no need at all to make a study of any dharma whatever. Just learn noninquiry and nonattachment. There is no mind that is born unless you seek for something. There is no mind that dies unless you are attached to something. To be without birth or death is Buddhahood. The eighty-four thousand gates to the dharma are there only to attract the students' attention.' This is only a teaching of ours, who are followers of Bodhidharma. All the teachings of the Great Vehicle [Mahayana] follow the same path.

"The *Lotus Sutra* says, 'Once at the Void-King's palace a craving for enlightenment awoke in me and in Ananda at the same time. He set about acquiring wide learning, whereas I devoted all my energies to practice. That is why I have attained enlightenment.' The *Surangama Sutra* says, 'When he saw the Buddha, Ananda cried out in grief, lamenting the fact that he could acquire no dharma power because he had devoted himself from the beginning to seeking knowledge only.' The *Sutra on Perfect Enlightenment* says, 'Whatever they may desire, students with no enlightenment who do not practice have no chance of attaining satori. They devote themselves to acquiring more knowledge, and in so doing simply make it harder than ever for themselves to see their true natures.' No one, even though he were to emit the light of wisdom as a result of reading many books, could compare his learning with Ananda's. It is much better to find the Buddha's way to enlightenment than to rely on scholarship. I am reluctant to speak of the sayings of the Patriarchs and to lecture on the sutras. Because what I really want is to make my students understand that the core of the teachings of the Buddha and the Patriarchs is never found in words and letters."

The monk inquired further: "Zen masters welcome the students of the first kind, and guide them with words and with direct presentations of mind, and they think most highly of those who have mastered both. So it is only natural that some gifted students should try to master mind and words at the same time. Do you say they are wrong?"

The Master answered, "One of our forerunners once said, 'Students who have had no glimpse of enlightenment would do better to study mind first rather than words. Those who have attained some enlightenment should study words first and then mind. You have called mind and words into question, but you know nothing of their real workings.' Another master said, 'Words polish mind and mind polishes words. It's best when you can use them freely, just as you please.' Do you really understand what he is saying? You must realize that the original state of satori has nothing to do with either of them, but that mind and words are separated simply as a means for teaching novices. Beginning students try to understand their teachers' words by analyzing them, and as a result they block their own way and lose the pointer that was guiding them toward satori. That is why the master said, 'Students who have had no glimpse of enlightenment would do better to study mind first rather than words.' On the other hand, someone who has attained enlightenment but has not mastered words will not be recognized as a master and will not be able to teach and guide students. So one may have a high regard for a perfect command of both mind and words without directing beginners to study mind and words at the same time."

The monk asked, "Zen masters these days give a koan to their disciples. This makes students study words, doesn't it?"

The Master answered, "No it doesn't. Yuan-wu said, 'Students who have just started Zen practice have no idea about it. So out of compassion the masters give them a koan as a signpost, so that the disciples can devote themselves to discovering oneness and dispelling random illusions, and to realizing finally that the Original Mind is not something that comes from outside. After that, all the koans turn out to be pieces of tile for knocking at the gate.' Do you consider this explanation of Yuan-wu's a deception? You must understand that Zen masters give their disciples a koan simply in order to guide them through the Gate of Satori into their own homes.

"Ta-hui used to cite a passage from some forerunner's sermon, to his own students: 'Don't try to use your intellect to grasp the truth. Don't just swallow everything that has been preached. And don't lock yourself up in the storehouse, where nothing happens.' This teaching is a sign of Ta-hui's deep, grandmotherly kindness. With it he blindfolds your eyes to let you see with your mind. You can understand from this that it is not words at all that Ta-hui wants you to study. Any students who have succeeded in returning their minds to the Original Silence by sitting on the zazen cushion but are still content with their marvelous skill with words are still a long way from the true study of mind.

"Yuan-wu says, 'The phrase "This mind, the Buddha" shows the truth as plainly as though it were seen through a wide-open gate. The other one, "No mind, no Buddha," forces one to face the truth directly and see through it. Without getting stuck in these words, pass right through them and then you will see clearly the whole mind of the Patriarchs, unveiled. If you get stuck in the words you will never attain enlightenment.' He says besides, 'If you are someone with great inborn genius there is no need to make a study of the old words and koans. When you wake up in the morning, make your mind clear and calm. Whatever has to be done then, do it as well as you can. Afterward, think it over carefully, and see what you have done and what it amounts to. When you have done these things thoroughly you will find yourself right there in the monastery of purity and no-happening.'

"These two masters set forth the very core of Zen practice. But most students these days fish words and dialogues of the masters out of books and store them in their heads until they have a chance to spar with others, using their cleverness in Zen talk, and they flatter themselves that they have attained the subtle way of the Patriarchs. But this is just what Yuan-wu calls conceit and delusion."

The monk questioned him again: "Those students who repeat Zen stories secondhand, and swallow hearsay and gossip, and convince themselves that they have attained satori are of course full of conceit and delusion. But there are some very gifted students who have penetrated to the core of Zen words. Are they not to be called people of satori?"

The Master answered, "Even those who have a keen insight into Zen words are to be called people accomplished in words but not in mind unless they have attained clear satori. As for those who merely pass on secondhand stories, swallow rumors, and gossip, they are not worth commenting on. A master says, 'Just grasp the essence, don't concern yourself with the results.' Attaining genuine satori is the essential. The manifestation of its great working is the result. It's like planting a tree. If the root goes deep, the leaves and flowers and fruit will be sure to flourish.

"Ta-hui says, 'In Zen practice generally, result is not everything.' And he tells this story:

Yun-kai Shou-chi on Cloud-Covered Mountain was a master known for his penetrating insight. One day the governor of the province came up the mountain and stopped for a rest at Talking-Void House. He asked, "What is the Talking-Void House?"

Shou-chi answered, "This is the Talking-Void House."

The governor was disappointed at this answer. So he sent for Yun-kai Chi-pen and asked him the same question.

Chi-pen answered, "I just preach the dharma at the House. Why am I supposed to talk about the void with my mouth?"

The governor was delighted, and appointed Chi-pen to preside over the monastery on Cloud-Covered Mountain.

If you compare the two, Chi-pen and Shou-chi, the

former is far behind the latter. But satori is not merely a matter of results.

"Pao-feng Ch'u-yuan on Treasure Peak was another master who had attained deep satori, but his handling of Zen dialogue was clumsy. Chueh-fan nicknamed him 'Yuan Fifty Liters.' Ch'u-yuan merely breathed with his mouth open until the fifty liters of rice came to a boil, and only then would he answer a question."

The monk asked, "If words and letters have a bad influence on students at the beginning, why did the masters in the past leave so many words of different kinds — the *daigo* [substitute words], *betsugo* [supplementary words], *nenko* [short comments], and *juko* [poetic comments] which are now widely used?"

The Master answered, "Those masters of discerning insight had a perfect command of words, and they used their skill to teach their disciples. Each word and phrase may show a different aspect of Zen, but each is no more than a means — like the woman's call for her maid, not for an errand but simply so that her lover would hear her voice and know that she was there inside the window. The masters' words did no harm to their students, and some bright ones grasped the essential beyond those words. But with the passage of time, misunderstandings inevitably occurred. Many stupid people came along, like the man who spent all his time watching the old stump into which a rabbit had run and killed itself—he was waiting for it to happen again. Or the one who dropped his sword into the current from his moving boat and marked the side of the boat to show where it fell, and then searched in the water underneath. Then every five hundred years or so a great master appears in the world who can wipe out all these accumulated evils. That is what is called 'breaking the deadlock' or 'family broken up, house ruined.'

"Once Yuan-wu, when he was living on Chia Mountain, prepared lectures for his disciples, called *Hsueh-tou's Hundred Koans with Verse Comments.* Later the lectures were compiled and published under the title of *The Blue Cliff Records.* But Fo-chien, a dharma brother, wrote to him reproachfully, saying, 'When I served Wu-tsu Fa-yen he encouraged us by saying, "Each of you, when you become a Buddha some day, a teacher of the world, be sure that you devote yourselves entirely to 'this matter'—I mean the attainment and deepening of satori." I was so impressed by his words that I have never forgotten them. I hear that you have added many comments to *Hsueh-tou's Verse Comments,* with a view to helping your students to understand. When I learned that, I could not help shedding tears. I thought that you were a man of true satori. Why on earth have you been doing such a thing? Why don't you show your disciples the one Original Truth that was there before Bodhidharma visited China? And so on. . . .' According to *Ta-hui's Discourses,* 'When my teacher read Fo-chien's letter he gave up the undertaking.'

"But some meddlesome fellows published Yuan-wu's lectures in book form and so they came into general use. Later, Ta-hui burned the printing blocks. That was an example of 'family broken up, house ruined.' In 1304, two hundred years after the blocks were burned, Chang Ming-yuan republished the book, which was then widely read. A man named Old Man San-chiao wrote a preface to it. He said, 'Someone asked me whether it would be better to keep the copies of *The Blue Cliff Records* or to burn them. I answered that either would be good. . . .' The writer of the preface maintains that there is a good reason for both of the contradictory things: for Yuan-wu's lectures and for Ta-hui's burning them. This official is ignorant of the fact that the masters' intention was neither to keep nor to burn the book.

"Before the days of Ma-tsu and Pai-chang, masters put much emphasis on *richi* and little on *kikan.* Later they paid a great deal of attention to practice and little to theoretical study. Later, in the days of Feng-hsueh and

Hsing-hua, they resorted to higher expressions of Zen experience, and this tendency made it more difficult to grasp their teachings. This is another example of 'breaking the deadlock.' After all, we should remember that the Patriarchs' aim is neither study nor practice, but that both are merely means, like the woman calling her maid for no errand. So the master says, 'If I meet someone who is ready for my dharma I will hand it on to that person. Otherwise, I will leave everything to the way of the world.' He adds, 'Face the Buddha's teachings as though they were the enemy you will never forgive, and then you may learn something of them.'"

The monk went on, "Well, then, would it be best to spend one's time in complete silence, without reading anything?"

The Master answered, "One master said, 'The truth can be attained neither by words nor by silence.' The patriarchs and the descendants of the Bodhidharma are not supposed to rely on words and letters. Is that supposed to mean that silence is to be preferred and words are to be avoided? On the contrary, the one thing they want is for students to see that the real truth lies neither in words nor in silence. Once this fact is clear to you, all the teachings of the Buddha and the Patriarchs are matters within your own house. So if you want to understand their teachings, please let go of whatever knowledge and wisdom you may have acquired up until now, and forgetting about yourself entirely, devote yourself completely to the one koan. Those students who are naturally gifted will not only go beyond koan study but will also escape falling into mere silence. They always go straight to the essential. Those are the ones who are unquestionably my disciples. Everything that I have said up until now is for their sake. I am unwilling to teach those scatterbrained students who have no sincere wish for the truth but only a restless urge to collect knowledge. But some who are aware of the unremitting law of cause and effect, and live a modest life, or who try to learn something from Zen monastery life, and practice to make something of their lives, may be able to accomplish a kind of Zen in their own way. I cannot turn aside from such people either.

"One of Pu-tai's 'Ten No-Uses' goes, 'If both practice and learning were to be abandoned, even priesthood would be meaningless.' This may reflect on what I have been saying. Lately some priests have turned their whole study to scriptures other than Buddhist. But there they really learn neither mind nor words. Do they in fact deserve to be called Zen priests? Such people have been dealt with already in a number of the sutras. Since they have become disciples of the Buddha, why do they pay no attention to his teachings?"

The monk's questions continued: "There are people who have learned Zen talk and flatter themselves that they have fully understood what is meant by 'Bodhidharma's reason for coming to China.' What makes you assume that they have not attained enlightenment?"

The Master answered, "Once a master said, 'Bodhidharma came to China from the west but he never preached a word of the dharma to anyone. All he did was to show that everyone without exception is endowed with the dharma and is already accomplished and perfect, and that there is not the slightest gap between each individual and the Buddha and the Patriarchs. Since everyone is no different from the Buddha and the Patriarchs, it is pointless to argue about superiority and inferiority between you and me. If someone is so conceited as to insist that he is enlightened but others are not, it is quite obvious that this person is not enlightened and has not understood the meaning of 'Bodhidharma's reason for coming to China from India.' Those who have grasped the mind of Bodhidharma know perfectly well that the sutra-studying school's theories of the relative and absolute, phenomena and noumena, and Zen's *richi* and *kikan* are after all nothing but fingers pointing at the moon, or tiles for knocking at the gate. Students get together nowadays to measure each other's fingers or to guess the dimensions of each other's piece of tile, and they manage to persuade themselves that they have attained satori. This is nothing but 'lip Zen.' How could we call people like this descendants of Bodhidharma?

"Ta-hui was a wandering monk in his youth, and he learned 'lip Zen.' He flattered himself that he had attained complete satori, but he realized at last that that was not true. He visited Yuan-wu and finally had his lumps of illusion smashed to pieces. After that he always spoke of his mistake as a way of warning his disciples. Today's students, too, must keep this teaching in mind. The masters with true insight hold out their hands to offer guidance, sometimes seizing their disciples, sometimes turning them loose, sometimes snatching everything away from them, sometimes giving them everything. They do it all as quickly and with as little trace as a flint spark or a flash of lightning. This is the art of the great masters, the art of blindfolding one's distracted eyes. Yung-chia says, 'Sometimes I say yes and sometimes no; nobody knows which beforehand. Upside down or right side up: even Heaven cannot predict.' Those who have not reached his level of satori but merely imitate the art of the masters deceive themselves and, what is worse, let loose an evil karma that spreads to many others. We must be very careful about this."

On Gardens and the Way

FROM *DIALOGUES IN THE DREAM*, SECTION 57

From ancient times until now there have been many who have delighted in raising up mounds of earth, making arrangements of stones, planting trees, and hollowing out watercourses. We call what they make "mountains and streams." Though all seem to share a common liking for this art of gardening, they are often guided by very different impulses.

There are those who practice the art of gardening out of vanity and a passion for display, with no interest whatever in their own true natures. They are concerned only with having their gardens attract the admiration of others.

And some, indulging their passion for acquiring things, add these "mountains and streams" to the accumulation of rare and expensive things that they possess, and end up by cherishing a passion for them. They select particularly remarkable stones and uncommon trees to have for their own. Such persons are insensible to the beauty of mountains and streams. They are merely people of the world of dust.

Po Lo-t'ien dug a little pool beside which he planted a few bamboos, which he cared for with love. He wrote a poem about them:

The bamboo — its heart is empty.
It has become my friend.
The water — its heart is pure.
It has become my teacher.

Those everywhere who love mountains and rivers have the same heart as Lo-t'ien and know the way out of the dust of the world. Some whose natures are simple are not attracted by worldly things, and they raise their spirits by reciting poems in the presence of fountains and rocks. The expression "a chronic liking for mist, incurably stricken by fountains and rocks" tells something about them. One might say that these are secular people of refined taste. Though they are in the world and without the spirit of the Way, this love of the art of gardens is nevertheless a root of transformation.

In others there is a spirit that comes awake in the presence of these mountains and rivers and is drawn out of the dullness of daily existence. And so these mountains and rivers help them in the practice of the Way. Theirs is not the usual love of mountains and rivers. These people are worthy of respect. But they cannot yet claim to be followers of the true Way because they still make a distinction between mountains and rivers and the practice of the Way.

Still others see the mountain, the river, the earth, the

grass, the tree, the tile, the pebble, as their own essential nature. They love, for the length of the morning, the mountain and the river. What appears in them to be no different from a worldly passion is at once the spirit of the Way. Their minds are one with the atmosphere of the fountain, the stone, the grass, and the tree, changing through the four seasons. This is the true manner in which those who are followers of the Way love mountains and rivers.

So one cannot say categorically that a liking for mountains and rivers is a bad thing or a good thing. There is neither gain nor loss in the mountain and the river. Gain and loss exist only in the human mind.

FROM *DIALOGUES IN THE DREAM*, SECTION 76

One time I went with seven or eight monks to West Lake, at the foot of Mount Fuji. It seemed to us that we had found a place of enchantment, and we could not help being moved by everything that we saw. We found a fisherman who lived by the lake there and got him to take us in the boat. Wherever the boat turned we saw another magnificent landscape. The monks could not contain their emotion, and kept exclaiming and clapping the side of the boat with their hands. The old man, who had lived by that lake all his life and seen the landscape every day from morning until evening, thought nothing of it. When he saw how excited the monks were he asked, "What is it? What are you so worked up about?" The monks answered, "We are admiring the beauty of this landscape, the views of this mountain and this lake." The old man was more puzzled than ever and he said, "You came all the way here just to see that?" He could not understand it.

I said to the monks, "If this old man asks us to explain to him what there is about this place that moves us, how can we tell him? If we point to the landscape of mountains and rivers and say to him that what moves us is just that, the old man will say that he has seen that for years and that there is nothing remarkable about it. On the other hand, if we try to change his mind by telling him that we are moved by something besides what he sees in front of him, he will think that what he sees is not what we care for at all, and that there is a further splendor beyond the West Lake."

The meaning of the "special transmission outside the scriptures" is just like this.

QUESTION: Teacher, what is the gate of the Law which you are really showing to others?
ANSWER: In Silla the sun shines at midnight!

This exchange is the conclusion of *Dialogues in the Dream* as it was edited by Musō's followers. Silla was an ancient Korean kingdom. The name had come to signify somewhere impossibly remote in time and place, and that is one of its meanings here.

Musō's Admonition

In some Zen temples in Japan this has been recited regularly as an exhortation ever since Musō's time.

I have three sorts of disciples. The best are those who resolutely give up all worldly relationships and devote themselves wholly to seeking and realizing their own true natures. The middle sort are not really earnest in Zen practice, and in order to find distraction from it prefer to read about it in books. The lowest are those who eclipse the light of their self-nature and do nothing but lick up the Buddha's spit. As for those students who care about nothing but non-Buddhist books and their own literary reputations, they are nothing more than laypeople with shaven heads. They are lower than the lowest. And lower still are those who spend their time doing nothing but eating and sleeping. Do they even deserve to be called black-robed monks? A Zen master once called them "robe-hangers" and "rice bags." They are not monks at all, and I will not let them come and go in the temple and subtemples, calling themselves my disciples. I will not even put them up for a visit and certainly would not let them stay to become followers of mine. This is the will left by this old monk. Don't blame me for not extending mercy and love to everyone. My one wish is for all students to see and correct their shortcomings and become worthy of the seeds and trees of the Way of the Patriarchs.

List of Names

After each name, occurrences in the text are noted by poem number or by w, for *West Mountain Evening Talk*; D, *Dialogues in the Dream*; or INTRO, "Introduction." Traditionally, Musō Soseki has been called Musō Kokushi; "kokushi" is an honorific title, "Teacher of the Nation." "Oshō" and "zenji" are also honorific titles to Zen masters, though priests are generally called "oshō" today.

ASHIKAGA MOTOUJI (1340–1367): one of Takauji's sons. (123)

ASHIKAGA TADAYOSHI (1306–1352): Ashikaga Takauji's brother. (INTRO, 73, 85)

ASHIKAGA TAKAUJI (1305–1358): founder of the Muromachi Shogunate (1336–1573). (INTRO, 75, 111)

ASHIKAGA YOSHIAKIRA (1330–1367): one of Takauji's sons and the second general of the Muromachi Shogunate. (124)

BUKKŌ ZENJI: Mugaku Sogen or Wu-hsueh Tsu-yuan (1226–1286): Chinese Zen master. Came to Japan and became the founder of Engaku-ji in Kamakura. Dharma grandfather. (90, w)

BUKKOKU ZENJI: Kōhō Ken'nichi (1256–1316): Bukkō Zenji's successor and Musō's teacher. (INTRO, w)

CHAO-CHOU: Chao-chou Ts'ung-shen (778–897): Chinese Zen master. (6, 34, 69, w)

CHUEH-FAN: Chueh-fan Hui-hung (1071–1128): editor of *Forest Life*. Chinese. (w)

DAISEN OSHŌ: Daisen Dōtsū (1265–1339): dharma friend. (8)

DŌGEN: Eihei Dōgen (1200–1253): founder of the Japanese Sōto Zen; famous for his *Shōbō Genzō* [*The Eye and Treasury of the True Law*]. (INTRO)

DOMPŌ SHŪŌ (D. 1401): disciple. (94)

FENG-HSUEH: Feng-hsueh Yen-chao (896–973): Chinese. (w)

FO-CHIEN: Fo-chien Hui-ch'in (1059–1117): Chinese. (w)

GASSAN SHŪSŪ (1331–1399): disciple. (35)

GEN: Kosen Ingen (1295–1374): dharma friend. Studied in Yuan China. (42, 79)

GEN'NŌ OSHŌ: Gen'nō Hongen (1281–1332): dharma brother. (31, w)

GIDŌ SHŪSHIN (1325–1388): major disciple. (63)

GO-DAIGO (1288–1339): emperor. (INTRO, 22)

GYOKUEN (dates unknown): Hosokawa Yoriyuki's wife. (71)

GYOKUGAN: see Ashikaga Motouji. (123)

HEIZAN ZENKIN (dates unknown): disciple. (126)

HŌGAI KŌON (D. 1363): disciple. (127)

HŌGO KŌRIN (D. 1373): dharma friend. Studied in Yuan China. (118)

HOSOKAWA YORIYUKI (1329–1392): warrior and feudal lord. (70)

HSIANG-YEN: Hsiang-yen Chih-hsien (D. 898): Chinese Zen master. Attained satori at the sound of a stone hitting a bamboo stalk. (21)

HSING-HUA: Hsing-hua Ts'un-chiang (830–888): Chinese. (w)

HSUEH-TOU: Hsueh-tou Ch'ung-hsien (980–1052): Chinese. (w)

HUANG-LUNG: Huang-lung Hui-nang (1002–1069): Chinese Zen master. (51)

HUANG-PO: Huang-po Hsi-yun (D. 856?): Chinese. (w)

HUI-NENG: Hui-neng Ta-chien (638–713): the Sixth Patriarch. Lived at Ts'ao Valley. Chinese. (INTRO, 61, 102, 111, 119, 121)

IKU: Genshō Shūiku (1321–1386): disciple. Studied in Yuan China. (44)

ISSAN KOKUSHI: I-shan I-ning (1248–1317): Chinese Zen master. Visited Japan and lived at Kenchō-ji and Engaku-ji. (INTRO, W)

KAN: Tsūsō Kōkan (dates unknown): disciple. (43)

KANSŌ SHUKAN (dates unknown): disciple. (120)

KEIGAN: see Hosokawa Yoriyuki. (70)

KENGAI OSHŌ: Kengai Kōan (1252–1331): dharma friend. (34)

KIHŌ SHIYŪ (dates unknown): disciple. (27)

KO: Reigaku Sōko (dates unknown): dharma friend. Studied in Yuan China. (98)

KŌAN FUSHŌ (dates unknown): disciple. (48)

KOBOKU JŌEI (dates unknown): disciple. (25)

KOGEN SHŌGEN (D. 1364): dharma friend. Studied in Yuan China. (121)

KŌGON (1313–1364): emperor. Became a Zen priest after retirement. (64)

KŌHŌ KEN'NICHI: see Bukkoku Zenji. (INTRO, W)

KOKEI REIBUN (dates unknown): disciple. (109)

KOSAN: see Ashikaga Tadayoshi. (73)

KYŪŌ FUKAN (1321–1410): disciple. Studied in Yuan China. (26)

LIN-CHI: Lin-chi I-hsuan (D. 867): Chinese Zen master, founder of the Rinzai (Lin-chi) sect. (60, W)

LIN HSIANG-RU (third century B.C.E.): famous statesman in the old China. (19)

MA-TSU: Ma-tsu Tao-i (707–786): Chinese Zen master. (39, w)

MEGHASHRI: fictitious character appearing in the Hua-yen (Kegon) sutra; one of the fifty-three saints and the first person visited by Sudhana. (20)

MOKUAN SHŪYU (1318–1373): disciple. (72)

MOKUŌ MYŌKAI (dates unknown): disciple. (122)

MUGOKU OSHŌ: Mugoku Shigen (1282–1359): major disciple. (74, 113)

MUHAN: see Kōgon. (64)

MYŌ: Mōzan Chimyō (1292–1366): dharma uncle. (80, 81)

NANG-YANG: Nan-yang Hui-chung (D. 775): Chinese Zen master. (44)

NINZAN: see Ashikaga Takauji. (75)

OLD MAN HO: see Chao-chou. (34, 69)

OLD MAN SAN-CHIAO (dates unknown): Ta-hui's dharma grandson; Chinese layman. (w)

PAI-CHANG: Pai-chang Huai-hai (720–814): Chinese Zen master. (w)

PAO-FENG CH'U-YUAN (dates unknown): Chinese Zen master. (w)

PO LO-T'IEN (772–846): famous poet in T'ang China. (D)

PU-TAI (D. 916): Chinese Zen layman. (w)

RINZAN OSHŌ: Reizan Dōin or Ling-shan Tao-yin (1255–1325): Chinese Zen master and dharma friend. Came to Japan in 1320. (5, 6, 7)

SAGAMI UMENOKAMI (dates unknown): minister of horses. (47)

SEIKEI TSŪTETSU (1300–1385): disciple. Studied in Yuan China. (119)

SEISETSU SHŌCHŌ: Ch'ing-cho Cheng-ch'eng (1274–1339): Chinese Zen master. Came to Japan in 1326. (40)

SHEN-KUAN: Hui-k'o (487–593): name of the Second Patriarch in his younger days. Showed his earnest wish to become Bodhidharma's disciple by cutting off one of his arms. (68, 77)

SHŌ: Kasan Sōshō (dates unknown): possibly a disciple. (83)

SHŌZAN SHŪNEN (dates unknown): disciple. (39)

SHUN'OKU MYŌHA (1311–1388): major disciple. Edited the *West Mountain Evening Talk*. (95)

SOHŌ PŌ (dates unknown): disciple. (46)

SUBHŪTI (dates unknown): the one of Shākyamuni's Ten Disciples who best understood emptiness. (30, 70)

SUDHANA: fictitious young boy in the Hua-yen sutra. Visits fifty-three saints seeking instruction and meets Meghashri first. (20, 99)

SŪZAN OSHŌ: Sūzan Kochū (1276–1345): dharma friend. Studied in Yuan China. (76, 77, 114)

TA-HUI: Ta-hui Tsung-kao (1089–1163): Chinese Zen Master. (w)

TAIHEI OSHŌ: Taihei Myōjun (1276–1327): dharma brother and one of Musō's best friends. (4, 11)

TAN-HSIA: Tan-hsia T'ien-jan (739–824): Chinese Zen master. (15)

TEKIAN HŌJUN (dates unknown): disciple. (129)

TENGAN OSHŌ: Tengan Ekō (1273–1335): dharma brother. Studied in Yuan China. (49)

TETSU: Daidō Myōtetsu (dates unknown): dharma brother. (82)

UNZAN CHIETSU (dates unknown): dharma friend. (41)

VIMALAKĪRTI (dates unknown): lay Buddhist in the days of Shākyamuni. The protagonist of the Vimalakīrti sutra. (122)

WU-TSU FA-YEN (1024–1104): Chinese Zen master. (w)

YUAN-WU: Yuan-wu K'o-ch'in (1063–1135): Chinese Zen master. (w)

YUNG-CHIA: Yung-chia Hsuan-chiao (665–713): Chinese Zen master, Hui-neng's disciple. (w)

YUN-KAI CHI-PEN (dates unknown): Chinese Zen master. (w)

YUN-KAI SHOU-CHI (1025–1115): Chinese Zen master. (w)

ZESSHŌ CHIKŌ (dates unknown): disciple. (128)

ZUIZAN: see Ashikaga Yoshiakira. (124)

Notes to the Poems

4 Taihei (in Japanese), literally "perfect peace."

6 Chao-chou once visited a hermit and said, "Hi, there." The latter held up his fist as his answer to the former. Then Chao-chou left the hut, saying, "The water's too shallow to anchor here." He then went to see another hermit, who also held up his fist. But this time Chao-chou nodded with affirmation. "Well, what's the difference?" This is a koan.

12 The Dragon Gate falls: the famous Yu-Gate falls in China. A legend relates the story of a carp that succeeds in climbing the falls and then turns into a dragon. Symbolically, the gateway represents success in one's career.

15 It is said that once Tan-hsia slept lying on the bridge leading to Lo-yang, to the surprise of the city official who discovered him.

17 In an old Chinese story, a man goes into the bottle with its owner, an old druggist on the street, and enjoys the land of wizards. (In Zen, this strange experience suggests that of satori.)

19 Lin was sent to the king of Ch'in, a neighboring country, because the latter proposed to exchange the noted flawless jewel owned by Lin's lord with the fifteen castles of Ch'in. But when Lin handed the jewel to the king, the latter broke his promise, pretending that he had forgotten his offer. Lin asked the king to return the jewel to him so that he could reveal its one hidden flaw. Actually the jewel had no flaw. Thus Lin kept the jewel

from falling into the enemy's hands and narrowly escaped with his life back to his country.

20 Sudhana visits fifty-three saints, seeking instruction. He wants to visit Meghashri, the very first teacher of the Buddhist truth, but looks for him in vain; seven days later he sees Meghashri walking on Another Summit. This is a koan.

22 The emperor is Go-Daigo.

25 "Dry Tree," *koboku* in Japanese: Koboku Jōei.

26 "Old Man in Retirement," *kyūō* in Japanese: Kyūō Fukan.

27 "Strange Peak," *kihō* in Japanese: Kihō Shiyū.

29 Nachi is noted for its falls; Kannon is the Japanese rendering of Avalokiteshvara, a bodhisattva of mercy, whose wish is to save the whole world.

34 Old Man Ho: Chao-chou. Cf. note to poem 6. Engaku-ji is called "Zuiroku-san" — literally, a mountain full of deer, which suggests a good omen.

35 "Moon Mountain," *gassan* in Japanese: Gassan Shūsū.

38 In *Lun-yü*, Confucius agreed with his disciple's words of joy in the passing spring.

39 "Laughing Mountain," *shōzan* in Japanese: Shōzan Shūnen. Ma-tsu once kicked at the leg of his disciple to lead him into satori.

40 Fukusan dormitory, the student hall built in Kenchō-ji in 1327. The "Great Master" suggests Seisetsu Shōchō and also Shākya-muni.

41 "Cloud Mountain," *unzan* in Japanese: Unzan Chietsu.

42 The "great death" is the complete death of one's own ego; from this once-and-for-all experience of emptiness starts a new Zen life.

44 Nang-yang once summoned his attendant monk three times, and the latter responded each time. The meaning of these three summonses and responses is a koan.

46 "Patriarch Peaks," *sohō* in Japanese: Sohō Pō.

47 "East Peak": layman Sagami Umenokami's dharma name.

48 "Old Hut," *koan* in Japanese: Kōan Fushō.

51 Huang-lung guided his students by the famous koan "Huang-lung's Three Barriers."

57 The Three Worlds: the world of desire, of the five senses; the world of form but of no desire; the world of neither form nor desire.

60 Lin-chi planted pine trees as a guidepost for the younger generation.

63 "Truth Hall," or the first truth gate; *gidō* in Japanese: Gidō Shūshin.

64 "No Precedent," *muhan* in Japanese: Emperor Kōgon's dharma name after retirement.

65 Long eyebrows: symbol of a great man of satori. "Have grown from your chin": Though logically nonsense, this is one of the typical expressions of the free workings of Zen.

69 Old Man Ho: Chao-chou. Cf. note for poem 6.

70 "Moon Tree Cliff," *keigan* in Japanese: Hosokawa Yoriyuki's dharma name.

71 "Gem Creek," *gyokuen* in Japanese: Hosokawa Yoriyuki's wife's dharma name.

72 "No-Word Hut," *mokuan* in Japanese: Mokuan Shūyu.

73 "Old Mountain," *kosan* in Japanese: Ashikaga Tadayoshi's dharma name.

74 "No End Point," *mugoku* in Japanese: Mugoku Shigen.

75 "Lover of Mountains," *ninzan* in Japanese: General Ashikaga Takauji's dharma name.

77 Sūzan (Mount Ch'ung) refers to the mountain where Bodhidharma lived. Shen-kuan stood buried in snow up to his waist, asking Bodhidharma's permission to be his disciple.

78 "Pure Sound Pavilion": Bon'non-kaku. "Riverside Temple": Rinsen-ji.

79 Erin-ji: literally, "Forest of Wisdom Temple."

80 Anzen-ji: literally, "Joy of Zen Temple."

81 Shōfuku-ji: literally, "Sacred Fortune Temple."

87 Rōhatsu, or December 8, is the day when Shākyamuni attained satori at the moment he saw the morning star. In celebration of it, each monastery holds a special intensive practice from December 1 to the morning of December 8.

90 Bukkō: literally, "Buddha's Light."

94 "The Fragrance of the Udumbara," *dompō* in Japanese: Dompō Shūō.

95 "House of Spring," *shun'oku* in Japanese: Shun'oku Myōha.

99 "Dragon of Heaven Temple": Tenryū-ji. "The Gate of Universal Light": Fumyō-kaku.

100 "Incomparable-Verse Valley": Zesshō-kei.

101 "Hall of the Guardian God": Reihi-byō.

102 "Hui-neng's Pond": Sōgen-chi.

103 "The Peak of the Held-Up Flower": Nenge-rei.

104 "The Bridge Where the Moon Crosses": Togetu-kyō.

105 "Three-Step Waterfall": Sankyū-gan.

106 "Cave of the Thousand Pines": Banshō-dō.

107 "Dragon-Gate House": Ryūmon-tei.

108 "Turtle Head Stupa": Kichō-tō.

109 "Tiger Valley," *kokei* in Japanese: Kokei Reibun.

111 General Ashikaga Takauji's residence. The Three God Mountains: the three legendary mountains (P'eng-lai, Fang-chang, and Ying-chou) of ancient China where hermit gods live.

118 "Ox Turned Loose," *hōgo* in Japanese: Hōgo Kōrin.

119 "Clear Valley," *seikei* in Japanese: Seikei Tsūtetsu.

120 "Old Man at Leisure," *kansō* in Japanese: Kansō Shukan.

121 "Ancient Origin," *kogen* in Japanese: Kogen Shōgen.

122 "Old Man of Few Words," *mokuō* in Japanese: Mokuō Myōkai. Vimalakīrti, in the dialogue between Manjushri and himself

concerning the dharma of nonduality, answers Manjushri with silence. In Zen this silence of his is compared to thunder.

123 "Jewel Cliff," *gyokugan* in Japanese: Ashikaga Motouji's dharma name.

124 "Joy Mountain," *zuizan* in Japanese: Ashikaga Yoshiakira's dharma name.

126 "Flat Mountain," *heizan* in Japanese: Heizan Zenkin.

127 "Beyond the World," *hōgai* in Japanese: Hōgai Kōon.

128 "Beyond Light," *zesshō* in Japanese: Zesshō Chikō.

129 "Hut in Harmony," *tekian* in Japanese: Tekian Hōjun.

130 The civil war (1336–1392) refers to the war between the two Ashikaga brothers, Takauji and Tadayoshi.

About the Translators

W.S. MERWIN's honors include the Bollingen Prize, two Pulitzer Prizes, the Aiken Taylor Award for Modern American Poetry (a Ford Foundation grant), the Ruth Lilly Poetry Prize, the PEN Translation Prize, the Shelley Memorial Award, the Wallace Stevens Award, and a Lila Wallace-Reader's Digest Writers' Award. He has also been awarded fellowships from The Academy of American Poets, the Guggenheim Foundation, the National Endowment for the Arts, and the Rockefeller Foundation. Merwin is a former Chancellor of The Academy of American Poets and has served as Special Consultant in Poetry to the Library of Congress in 1999–2000 and as Poet Laureate in 2010–2011.

SŌIKU SHIGEMATSU is a priest of the Myoshin-ji branch of Rinzai School of Zen Buddhism; abbot of Shōgen-ji Temple in Shimizu-ku, Shizuoka; and author and translator of books and essays on Zen that were instrumental in spreading interest in Zen literary tradition to the West in the latter half of the twentieth century. He won the Jerome J. Shestack Poetry Prize from *The American Poetry Review* in 1987.

 Poetry is vital to language and living. Since 1972, Copper Canyon Press has published extraordinary poetry from around the world to engage the imaginations and intellects of readers, writers, booksellers, librarians, teachers, students, and donors.

WE ARE GRATEFUL FOR THE MAJOR SUPPORT PROVIDED BY:

THE PAUL G. ALLEN
FAMILY FOUNDATION

amazon.com

the
P●INT
WHERE LESS IS MORE

golden
lasso

Lannan

THE MAURER FAMILY
FOUNDATION

NATIONAL
ENDOWMENT
FOR THE ARTS

WASHINGTON STATE
ARTS COMMISSION

Anonymous
Arcadia Fund
John Branch
Diana and Jay Broze
Beroz Ferrell & The Point, LLC
Mimi Gardner Gates
Gull Industries, Inc.
on behalf of William and Ruth True
Mark Hamilton and Suzie Rapp
Carolyn and Robert Hedin
Steven Myron Holl
Rhoady and Jeanne Marie Lee
Maureen Lee and Mark Busto
Brice Marden
New Mexico Community Foundation
H. Stewart Parker
Penny and Jerry Peabody
Joseph C. Roberts
Cynthia Lovelace Sears and Frank Buxton
The Seattle Foundation
Charles and Barbara Wright
The dedicated interns and faithful
volunteers of Copper Canyon Press

To learn more about underwriting Copper Canyon Press titles,
please call 360-385-4925 ext. 103

The Chinese character for poetry is made up of two parts: "word" and "temple." It also serves as pressmark for Copper Canyon Press.

About one hundred years after Musō wrote his last poem, Nicolas Jenson was cutting type for the flourishing publishing trade in Venice. Specimens of Jenson's work inspired the digital typeface Adobe Jenson, by Robert Slimbach, used throughout this book. Book design by VJB/Scribe. Printed on archival-quality paper at McNaughton & Gunn.